The Ultimate MBA

For Charlotte

The Ultimate MBA

Meaningful Biblical Analogies for Business

Gary L. Moreau

Augsburg Books
MINNEAPOLIS

Contents

Introduction

I've spent twenty-five years in the business world, nearly half of that time as president or CEO of some very well-known and respected companies. In that time, I came to the realization that two premises I had long accepted about business were false. This book deals with both of them.

The Quandary of Compartmentalization

The first has to do with the modern notion that in order to be professional in business, you have to separate your personal life from your career. Like a lot of Christians in business, I've long struggled with the compartmentalization of my faith and my job. How can I develop a relationship with God on a part-time basis? Does business really have to be all profit and no compassion?

To get around this quandary, for many years I rationalized that as long as I didn't violate my Christian values while at the office, I could pursue both my relationship with God and my desire to be a successful business executive on parallel tracks. I now realize that I couldn't and I didn't have to.

In the aftermath of Enron, WorldCom, and the rest of the long list of sordid corporate sagas of recent years, a great many people have suggested that we need to put Christian values back in the corner office. I have no quarrel with that. I believe that we should seek to have Christian values everywhere—in our schools, our political institutions, and our businesses.

I also know, however, that values-driven leadership is not enough. Corporations are institutions, not persons. They don't have values; they have processes. Unless those processes are built on sound Christian doctrine, the values of the man or the woman at the top will have limited impact on how the institution behaves.

People respond to what you do, not to what you say. In the workplace, employees respond to what you inspect, not to what you expect. For example, even if you have repeatedly told the people working for you that you expect them to be honest and forthright in all communication, you can rest assured that you won't get a complete and accurate reporting the next time something goes wrong if you fired the last person to deliver bad news.

Most of the executives I've worked with over the years are decent, honest people. Many of the Christians among them, however, know in the pit of their stomach that integrity isn't enough. Even the honest and compassionate executive instinctively senses a missing link between the hope and charity of his Christian perspective and the realities of his business existence. As one executive put it, "I feel energized and enthusiastic on Sunday and deflated and overwhelmed on Monday."

It's a lose-lose situation for the company and the individual. As I'll demonstrate in the chapters that follow, there is no way to be successful in business over the long haul without adhering to the teachings of the Bible. I don't mean in some vague, conceptual way. I mean that God has laid it all out for us in the Bible, and every business book written since the Bible can be safely ignored.

All business is voluntary. It is not an end in itself. We participate in commerce as a matter of convenience, not as part of

God's plan for us. God, I believe, has nothing against business or profit. Frankly, I don't think God cares about business one way or the other. God cares only about the people who conduct it and about what they do with the success they realize.

Profit is not a spiritually dirty word. Profit is not, however, a legitimate purpose for business, any more than breathing is a legitimate reason for living. To the extent that we are personally pro-business or anti-business, we make business into something it is not. Business is life, but life is not business.

The Bible contains all we need to know about either life or business. Just as the Bible teaches us how to live a full and satisfying life, it inescapably teaches us how to conduct a successful business and how to have a rewarding and fulfilling career. The recipe for both is the same—a personal relationship with God.

The compartmentalization of our work and our faith deprives Christians in the most fundamental way. God has a plan for all of us, and I guarantee it doesn't include sitting in an office trying to figure out how to hit your budget, even if you're honest and upright in doing so. Business success may be the medium by which we realize and attain God's plan for us, but it is not the plan itself. By separating faith and work, we deprive ourselves of the incredible opportunity God has given us to know him and to realize our true personal potential, an achievement without which we cannot know true fulfillment.

False Complexity

Fortunately, being a good Christian and a good businessperson is far easier than we have been led to think. This brings me to the second realization that led me to write this book. We—and I include myself as a business leader—have made business far more complicated than it really is. We fail so often in business not because it is complex and difficult, but because we become obsessed with deciphering complexity that isn't there.

Much of the complexity we fabricate in business is falsely attributed to change. We can't get through a day without talking about how fast things are changing, how the pace of change is actually accelerating. Virtually all of that change, however, is superficial. The truths of the Bible—which are the truths of every facet of life, including business—are timeless.

In fact, little about business has changed since the first deal was done. The story of Adam and Eve in the Garden of Eden can teach us everything we need to know about marketing. And the story of Cain and Abel clearly demonstrates what it takes to run a successful enterprise.

Business people, however, have created an entirely distinct culture and language. We like to segment, categorize, and pre-qualify everything. We delude ourselves into thinking that a well-chosen and facilitated focus group will tell us what products to make or that sound product positioning is a function of adequate market research. We test, we analyze, and, often, we fail.

We have over-complicated business, I believe, because too many of us in business have not found fulfillment in our personal lives. As a result, we have created a fantasy world in which we can be smart and powerful and accomplished without having to come to grips with our lack of personal fulfillment. Because we lack personal fulfillment to the extent that we lack a relationship with God, until that relationship is a strong and growing one we are motivated to falsely believe that we can find fulfillment in a world—the world of business—that is somehow disconnected from God.

There is, however, no reality other than God's reality. We cannot toil in a spiritual vacuum and expect to find any meaningful satisfaction. If we try to do so, we dehumanize ourselves and trivialize our existence. That is the reality behind our dispirited and broken souls as we labor, day after day, separated from God in a world we have invented in order to remain apart from God.

The Bible and Business

The Bible is God's gift to us. In it, God has told us everything we need to know to know him and, in so doing, to know ourselves. Nothing is left out. If it's not there, it's not worth knowing. If it is, it most definitely is worth knowing. There is no fluff in the Bible.

In the next twelve chapters I will discuss twelve biblical stories. What these biblical stories say about business is only a variation on what they say about faith and personal fulfillment. Even those who never set foot inside an office building, factory, or small business establishment, therefore, will find something in this book to apply and use in the quest for a more fulfilling life through a relationship with God and his son, Jesus Christ.

I want to emphasize that my interpretation of each of these stories is not intended to be all-inclusive or doctrinally precise. I am not a theologian. I am not a scholar. I am simply a man—a businessman—who looks to the Bible for guidance on how to live a life that will bring me closer to God and the realization of his plan for me.

In the end, the way to align what we believe and what we do for a living is to appreciate that the Bible can be interpreted and applied at many levels. In fact, the Bible covers every facet of life. The same parables that guide each of us in our spiritual journey are the parables that can and should guide us in our work. Our faith and our work are merely two facets of the all-encompassing life God has granted each of us. While the interpretations we apply to each aspect of our life may seem quite distinct and different, they are different in appearance only.

It might be helpful to think of these different biblical interpretations as the different outfits we might wear on different occasions. Each outfit has a very distinct look, but doesn't change the person inside. Each biblical interpretation, similarly, is one variation on the fundamental, unchanging truths of the Bible. The fundamental truths remain the same, even as we apply them to various aspects of life.

I assure you that you have never heard or read these twelve biblical passages interpreted as I have interpreted them here. That's not to say that other interpretations you may be familiar with are wrong. My intent is not to substitute my interpretations for any others, but to demonstrate a very real connection between faith and career that has been previously overlooked.

Many business authors have attempted to find commonalities between successful companies and among successful business leaders. In truth, they have little in common other than their success. The commonalities "discovered" reflect little more than the common denominator of the authors' definition of success.

My definition of success is a very simple one—personal fulfillment. We can realize personal fulfillment only if life has purpose, and life can have purpose only if we live it in the context of faith and spirituality. The one thing all successful people do share is an appreciation of the interconnectedness of each facet of life and an unwavering desire to know God. With that understanding and commitment, we have everything it takes to unlock the eternal truths of the ultimate textbook on every subject—the Bible.

Chapter 1.

The Importance
of Choice

Adam and Eve in the Garden of Eden

Now the serpent was more crafty than any of the wild animals the Lord God had made. He said to the woman, "Did God really say, 'You must not eat from any tree in the garden'?"

The woman said to the serpent, "We may eat fruit from the trees in the garden, but God did say, 'You must not eat fruit from the tree that is in the middle of the garden, and you must not touch it, or you will die.'"

"You will not surely die," the serpent said to the woman. "For God knows that when you eat of it your eyes will be opened, and you will be like God, knowing good and evil."

When the woman saw that the fruit of the tree was good for food and pleasing to the eye, and also desirable for gaining wisdom, she took some and ate it. She also gave some to her husband, who was with her, and he ate it. Then the eyes of both of them were opened, and they realized they were naked; so they sewed fig leaves together and made coverings for themselves.

Then the man and his wife heard the sound of the Lord God as he was walking in the garden in the cool of the day, and they hid from the Lord God among the trees of the garden. But the Lord God called to the man, "Where are you?"

He answered, "I heard you in the garden, and I was afraid because I was naked; so I hid."

And he said, "Who told you that you were naked? Have you eaten from the tree that I commanded you not to eat from?"

The man said, "The woman you put here with me—she gave me some fruit from the tree, and I ate it."

Then the Lord God said to the woman, "What is this you have done?"

The woman said, "The serpent deceived me, and I ate."

. . . The Lord God made garments of skin for Adam and his wife and clothed them. And the Lord God said, "The man has now become like one of us, knowing good and evil. He must not be allowed to reach out his hand and take also from the tree of life and eat, and live forever." So the Lord God banished him from the Garden of Eden to work the ground from which he had been taken. After he drove the man out, he placed on the east side of the Garden of Eden cherubim and a flaming sword flashing back and forth to guard the way to the tree of life (Genesis 3:1-13; 21-24).

In Genesis 2 the Bible introduces us to Adam and Eve, the first man and woman. They live in the beautiful and lush Garden of Eden, where God has provided everything they need to lead an eternal life of simple pleasure. As we learn in Genesis 3, however, at the urging of the serpent, first Eve and then Adam do the one thing God forbade them to do. They eat the fruit from the tree of knowledge of good and evil.

God discovers their transgression and they are banished from Eden. With acquisition came loss. With the knowledge of good and evil came mortal lives complete with the toil and suffering we all endure from time to time.

Conscious Choice

Whether you believe this was the fall of man or the birth of free will, one thing is irrefutable: Adam and Eve made a voluntary choice. There were alternatives. There was plenty of other food around the Garden of Eden. They didn't have to pick the fruit of the tree of knowledge of good and evil. But they did. They made a conscious decision and acted upon it.

Life can be endured without much effort on our part. We can only truly live by choice, however. Faith, I believe, is an essential ingredient of living life to its fullest and requires conscious choice. While faithful Christians are sometimes portrayed by those who do not understand us as being unable or unwilling to think for ourselves, just the opposite is true. Faith is not blind acceptance; it is, in reality, the most conscious choice any of us will ever make.

Although I have always considered myself a Christian, I didn't realize true faith until I was well into my forties. It's not that I didn't believe in God or accept Jesus as my Savior. I went to church. I even became a deacon of the Presbyterian Church. I just didn't realize the opportunity for fulfillment and sheer joy that real faith could bring.

My eyes were opened by the simple message of a teaching pastor at the Kensington Community Church in Troy, Michigan. My wife and I were living in nearby Rochester at the time and had been scouting the area for a place of worship, so we stopped by one fateful Sunday morning. Kensington is a large church modeled after Willow Creek and originally affiliated with the Evangelical Presbyterian Church. They have several teaching pastors on staff, two of them at the time named Dave. (My wife and I kept their identities straight by referring to them as "blonde Dave" and "bald Dave," for what would be self-evident reasons if you met them.) It was "blonde Dave," Dave Nelson, who was giving the lesson on the Sunday we dropped in for the first time.

Dave, who claimed to be petrified of heights and had never so much as considered jumping out of an airplane before, had, in preparation for this lesson, taken a video crew along on his first skydive. Dave's lesson, reinforced by his example, was simple: If you want to have a relationship with God, you have to let go. You cannot *will* your faith; you must make a conscious choice to release your grip and let God demonstrate his love for you.

For me, it was the real beginning of my spiritual journey. I made the choice to let go and let God show me the way. I didn't give in or give up. I didn't fall into subservience. I *chose* to follow Jesus Christ. It wasn't a process of sacrificing my individuality, but a process of exerting it, of thinking for myself, and choosing to believe.

Choice and Motivation in Business

A business that is successful over the long term must have customers that choose to buy its product or service. A business that relies on willing the customer into submission will ultimately fail. It will most certainly not realize its true potential. As in faith, customers cannot be truly committed customers until they choose to be.

Choice has two ingredients. The first is the presence of alternatives. The second is action. The provider of a particular product or service must put something that is normally at rest (the customer) into motion. Then the customer must be persuaded to take action by choosing one product or service from among the alternatives.

Most companies spend a lot of time and effort trying to understand the needs and desires of customers. It sounds logical enough. After all, don't we buy things to satisfy a need or desire? Yes, but satisfying a need or desire is not enough. It does us little good as businesspersons if customers satisfy their need or desire by buying someone else's product or service.

Alternatives exist even when they seem not to. Until recently, most of us didn't have much choice when it came to buying local phone service, for example. But we always had the alternative of not having a phone. This may not be considered an acceptable alternative today, but that's a reflection of priorities, not need.

Getting back to the Garden of Eden, let's examine the topic of motivation. What if the serpent had merely pointed out that the fruit from the tree of knowledge of good and evil would satisfy Eve's physical need to eat, or that it contained more fiber or nutrients than the other fruit? Would she have chosen to violate God's directive not to eat the fruit of that particular tree? Probably not. She had plenty of acceptable alternatives.

She was motivated by the potential for access to knowledge. She and Adam could survive by eating any of the other fruit, but they would know good and evil only by eating the fruit of that one particular tree. And so they did. They didn't do it out of physical hunger or because they just happened to be in the neighborhood. They did it by choice, to gain knowledge that could be gained in no other way.

Needs and desires are often secondary motivations. Primary motivators are those that cause customers to choose to act, and to choose one product or service over another. For a business to succeed, therefore, it must do more than satisfy customers' needs or desires. It must satisfy their primary motivation. Motivation drives choice, and choice initiates the action on which a business's fate will turn.

Secondary Motivations

Let's look at a product that most of us buy from time to time—the automobile. What drives our purchase of cars and trucks? For starters, we need transportation. We need to get to work, to school, and to the store. There are alternatives, however. We could walk. We could buy a motorcycle or a bicycle. We could use public transportation.

These aren't the alternatives the car companies worry about, however. The alternatives they worry about are the products offered by the other car companies. Why? Because they know that most of us don't consider doing without a car to be a real option. For now, they're right. Should gasoline prices increase tenfold, however, consumers may realize that automobiles, like cell phones and DVD players, are a choice, not a necessity.

We also buy cars for identity. In our car-based culture, the automobile we drive is symbolic of who we are. It's a proxy for our success and the way in which we want others to think of us. In fact, few cars are bought today strictly on the basis of their ability to meet our transportation needs. That's why few SUVs ever leave the paved road and the beds of most pickup trucks never carry a load of plywood.

So what motivates us to buy one vehicle instead of another? There are occasions when our transportation needs change, and the first car manufacturer to satisfy these new needs is able to establish meaningful competitive advantage. The minivan is an excellent example. When Chrysler pioneered the category in 1986, there was a transportation need that was generally going unfulfilled—suburban families with kids in car seats and lots of gear. The invention of the child car seat and a changing lifestyle that seemed to put kids perpetually on the go essentially changed the definition of the family's transportation need.

The growth of the SUV category, on the other hand, wasn't so much a reflection of changing needs as it was a reflection of changing consumer identity desires. Few people actually needed the functionality that differentiated the SUV class. They just liked what the vehicle said about them.

The minivan and the SUV are two examples of new products that met a need or desire better than the competition did, providing valuable differentiation for the early entrants. They were analogous to the fruit of the tree of knowledge of good and evil. There were no close alternatives.

In some product categories, however, needs don't change all that often, and even when they do, competitors eventually figure it out. At a time when global out-sourcing is readily available and most production technology is now developed by independent third parties, competitors can generally get into new markets pretty quickly, giving the pioneer a relatively short period of real differentiation. This process is often described as the commoditization of innovation, but it starts with changing customer needs.

Why did Eve desire to see as God sees, to understand good and evil? That's a good topic for a Bible study group. I don't pretend to know the correct answer. Perhaps she gave in to temptation. Perhaps she was being taught a lesson (i.e., free choice) that couldn't be taught in any other way. Whatever the reason, the fruit of the tree of knowledge of good and evil was the fruit of choice on that particular occasion because it was the only fruit that offered what Eve believed she desired and was motivated enough to act on.

What happens when no new needs or desires emerge? In today's marketplace, profits typically get harder to come by. To continue the automotive example, Chrysler, now part of DaimlerChrysler, is far less profitable today because most other manufacturers offer minivans and SUVs, giving consumers a range of choices.

So what do you do when you're in an industry in which few new needs and desires are emerging at the moment? Ideally, everyone in the industry would take a time out. Every company keeps the customers it has and profit margins are sustained. But that, of course, isn't ever going to happen. It is the curse of every business to think it is better than its competitors and that it can take away some of their business. Swords are drawn and the end result is that everyone's margins are hacked to pieces.

The most common response is to try to stimulate desire or accelerate the fulfillment of need by lowering the price. Sometimes price reduction makes sense. Airlines, for example, know that nearly all of their costs are fixed; an empty seat costs as much as one with a body in it once the plane takes off. Any revenue they take for that seat is incremental.

In the longer term, however, lowering price to stimulate desire or accelerate need is suicidal unless you can lower your costs commensurately or a competitor goes out of business. Given the bankruptcy laws currently on the books, however, the true knockout punch is rare. Often, you just push the pain you inflicted on your competitor back onto its creditors.

The other problem with using price to drive sales is that it's seldom a net motivator. If you're just accelerating sales, at some point you'll obviously have to settle accounts. Even taking market share is of little long-term value unless it allows you to reduce costs in line with your aggressive pricing. Otherwise, at some point you'll have to give up your aggressive pricing or go out of business.

More often than not, aggressive pricing is actually counter-productive. The simple reason is that pricing can distort reality—or our perception of it—and lead us to build capacity that we can't sustain at acceptable profit margins. The automotive and airline industries are good examples. Both built excess capacity, in part, because their aggressive pricing tactics caused them to misread fundamental demand.

The only time that pricing is a net motivator is when a lower price causes the customer to make a purchase he or she otherwise would not make—now or ever. I may, for example, decide to fly to Orlando because the price is just too good to pass up. Still, pricing is not the only motivator. I wouldn't fly somewhere only because of a cheap fare. I have to have some prior reason to want to go there or even a free ticket won't motivate me to take the journey.

Primary Motivation

In the story of Adam and Eve, pricing played no role in Eve's decision to eat the fruit of the tree of knowledge of good and evil. God wasn't having a sale. In fact, Eve chose the fruit knowing that there would be a high price to pay. How much higher could the price have been than expulsion from the Garden of Eden?

Eve's action was initiated by a motivation more fundamental than price. She was seeking access to knowledge, to see as God sees, to know good and evil. In fact, access to knowledge is one of only four fundamental or primary motivations to all commerce. They are:

Access to Knowledge

When we are sick, we have a need/desire to be cured. We go to the doctor, however, because he or she is the one who went to medical school. We have a reasonable expectation that the doctor has acquired the knowledge to cure us. If we didn't, we might be inclined to try the grocery store first. It's probably closer. And the doctor would lose a potential patient despite our need/desire.

Cost Avoidance

With some effort, we might be able to figure out the way to convert crude oil into gasoline for our car. Chances are we won't want to, however. The up-front cost is huge. It's the kind of investment that needs to be spread over a large base of customers.

Convenience

Acquiring the knowledge to grow our own food would be easy, and the up-front costs would be minimal. But given the convenience of going to the grocery store, thinking about it is as far as most people ever get.

)me things most of us just aren't equipped to do. I
a picture or sing a song. If I enjoy those things,
ᴜ.ᴄ̲ I have to go to someone who has the talent I lack.
New technology is just a variation on the same theme.

In our automotive example, a car buyer is obviously motivated
by all four primary motivations to varying degrees. The challenge the automotive industry faces is establishing sustainable
differentiation, satisfying the four primary motivations in a
way its competitors don't and can't. Let's look at each one.

In the first case, access to knowledge is a variation of
anticipated quality and reliability. As consumers, we assume
that each of the car companies has the knowledge to fulfill our
transportation need or it wouldn't be in business. We do
believe some will do it more reliably than others, however,
and it's no surprise that those companies (for example, Toyota
and Honda) continue to grow and prosper despite the price
wars that have recently dominated the industry.

In terms of cost avoidance, price is obviously important to
most car buyers. A lower price doesn't help the company,
however, unless it reflects a lower cost. It may buy some time,
but it is only delaying the inevitable if it can't reduce its costs
and/or find a way to satisfy one or more of the other primary
motivators in a way the others don't.

Nobody in the automotive industry has figured out the
convenience motivator. Saturn tried, with its no-hassle pricing and low-key selling culture, but it never really had the
breadth of product to gauge consumer response. Finding an
alternative to the existing hard-sell dealer model won't be
easy for the American auto manufacturers, but if one company does it will have a real leg up, assuming it is competitive in terms of the other primary motivators.

That's why the Internet failed to fundamentally change
the automotive selling model. Buying a car on the Internet

isn't all that convenient. You can shop in your pajamas but you can't take a test drive or drive away with your purchase. And the Internet doesn't provide the same access to knowledge that the dealer does. Sure, you can read all of a car's features and specifications online, but actually seeing and sitting in a car provides access to knowledge that you simply can't acquire through a two-dimensional screen image.

The car companies do spend a great deal of money on innovation. Innovation, though, is a multifaceted issue. Of and by itself it does little to move the profit needle. It has to be relevant, cost effective and, ideally, sustainable.

Do you want to access your E-mail while driving to work? The car companies are betting you do. Focus group participants have undoubtedly told them they would, but the companies won't know for sure until the investment is already made. The same is true for satellite radio and wireless concierge services. Are they relevant? Time will tell.

Innovation always comes with a price tag. Electronic navigation clearly satisfies a primary motivation—access to information—but it isn't the only alternative available. Many motorists are content to consult a map or ask for directions until the cost of the electronic alternative drops significantly.

Even if an innovation is relevant and cost-effective, however, it will be of little value if it's fleeting. And it probably is. For a variety of reasons beyond the scope of this book, less and less innovation occurs within the companies that apply it. More often than not, innovation today is developed by entrepreneurs who have easier access to capital, giving them less reason to share the spoils with a corporate employer, or by established third party suppliers who can spread the development cost among multiple users.

That's both a plus and a minus for the non-innovator. The plus is that you won't be trumped in the marketplace by an innovative competitor. You can probably buy the same innovation. The minus is that the innovator will probably force all of its competitors to follow suit, for that same reason, and you won't want to be the only one left out.

The automotive industry, in short, competes largely on secondary needs and desires. We're told about the horsepower and the leather seats. We're told about the handling, or about how the manufacturer would like us to perceive the handling. We see beautiful, hip people getting in and out of cars. We're treated to upbeat rock music. And we're shown professional drivers on closed courses driving in ways few of us will ever try. In short, we're shown and told a lot of things that have little to do with the four primary motivators of all commerce.

So we ultimately react to the current sale or below-market financing or rebates or subsidized leases, all of which are just dressed-up versions of price. It is no surprise that domestic auto companies are selling a lot of vehicles, but no one is making much money. No one will until someone establishes superior knowledge (i.e., quality), a meaningfully lower cost of production, a more convenient selling model, and/or innovation in functionality or design that is relevant, cost-effective, and sustainable.

Virtually every great company that is consistently successful over a long period of time has found a way to tap into one of the four primary motivators in a way its competitors do not. No one needed another place to shop when Wal-Mart launched a dynasty on the basis of cost avoidance and convenience. Sony excels in a brutal marketplace with premium pricing by giving us access to the knowledge of Sony engineers and the innovation that flows from them. McDonalds gives us convenience. Disney gives us entertainment we're not equipped to create ourselves.

Enron, Global Crossing, and Tyco, on the other hand, satisfied none of the four primary motivators. Their early success was a product of financial engineering and captivating salesmanship. Like so many of the failed dotcoms, they looked to build a better mousetrap before it was determined if there were any mice.

Needs and desires are subordinate to primary motivations. The most successful companies aren't those that best satisfy a need; they are those companies that fulfill a need that aligns with the primary motivations of the customer. There was no money in the Garden of Eden. Money is nothing more than a method of scorekeeping. A successful business will generate money, but no form of it will create a successful business.

Remember, all business is voluntary. No one made Eve eat the fruit of the tree of good and evil. And no one will make customers buy a product or service. That decision is theirs; it is a matter of choice. You have to give them a reason to choose and, more importantly, a reason to choose to buy it from *you*.

For Further Reflection

What motivates your customer to buy your product or service?

Why are the companies you most admire successful?

How do the four primary motivators apply to some of the purchases you make?

Do you let the serpents influence you? Explain.

What are your true needs?

Do you believe you always have choice? Why or why not?

Do you try to obey God? Describe the ways you do or do not.

How does your job contribute to satisfying customer motivations?

What role does money play in business?

Would you eat the fruit of the tree of knowledge of good and evil even if God forbade it? Discuss your reasons.

Chapter 2.

Doing the Right Thing

Cain and Abel

Adam lay with his wife Eve, and she became pregnant and gave birth to Cain. She said, "With the help of the Lord I have brought forth a man." Later she gave birth to his brother Abel.

Now Abel kept flocks and Cain worked the soil. In the course of time Cain brought some of the fruits of the soil as an offering to the Lord. But Abel brought fat portions from some of the firstborn of his flock. The Lord looked with favor on Abel and his offering, but on Cain and his offering he did not look with favor. So Cain was very angry, and his face was downcast.

Then the Lord said to Cain, "Why are you angry? Why is your face downcast? If you do what is right, will you not be accepted? But if you do not do what is right, sin is crouching at your door; it desires to have you, but you must master it."

Now Cain said to his brother Abel, "Let's go out to the field." And while they were in the field, Cain attacked his brother Abel and killed him.

Then the Lord said to Cain, "Where is your brother Abel?"

"I don't know," he replied. "Am I my brother's keeper?"

The Lord said, "What have you done? Listen! Your brother's blood cries out to me from the ground. Now you are under a curse and driven from the ground, which opened its mouth to receive your brother's blood from your hand. When you work the ground, it will no longer yield its crops for you. You will be a restless wanderer on the earth."

Cain said to the Lord, "My punishment is more than I can bear. Today you are driving me from the land, and I will be hidden from your presence; I will be a restless wanderer on the earth, and whoever finds me will kill me."

But the Lord said to him, "Not so; if anyone kills Cain, he will suffer vengeance seven times over." Then the Lord put a mark on Cain so that no one who found him would kill him. So Cain went out from the Lord's presence and lived in the land of Nod, east of Eden (Genesis 4:1-16).

In this passage from the book of Genesis we learn the tragic story of Cain and Abel, the first two sons of Adam and Eve. Cain worked the soil and Abel kept flocks. When each prepared an offering for God, God looked with favor upon Abel, but not Cain. Cain became angry and murdered his brother, and God cursed Cain to a life of fruitless toil and restless wandering.

It's a story with personal and business relevance at many levels. It's a story of mistaken focus, of being preoccupied with the results of our work when it's the way we work and the purpose of our work that really matter. It's good to have a destination, as long as you recognize that when it comes to life—and business—the journey is more than the means to the end. The journey defines the destination. Success is all about doing the right thing, not making the right offering.

Results and the "Right Thing"
When things don't go as we plan, either in our business or our personal lives, the solution to our trouble lies in introspection and self-analysis, not reactive aggression. It's easy to become preoccupied with our perceived competitors, to

look for someone else to blame, to see solutions in offensive plots and schemes, rather than re-dedicate ourselves to doing the right thing and standing firm against the temptations of blame and envy.

Abel had little to do with God's disfavor toward Cain. His disfavor had nothing to do with the nature of the offering or with favoritism toward Abel. God's favor is not a zero-sum game. There is plenty of God's favor for all who do as Abel did—the right thing. The same goes for the rewards of commerce.

God gave us the Ten Commandments to guide our behavior. We will not abide by them, however, if that is all we set out to do. We are incapable of a sinless life without God's help. There is no immoral behavior that we are capable of avoiding through sheer discipline. We can only choose to follow the right path and that path will lead us to the result we desire.

Both Cain and Abel desired the grace of God. For Cain, however, the desire was all he had, so when his plan didn't pan out, he blamed it on Abel. Abel, on the other hand, focused on doing the right thing, on maintaining his relationship with God. Abel's success in achieving his objective was a function of the approach he took, not the outcome he desired.

It all comes back to choice. Abel made the choice to do the right thing—win, lose, or draw. Cain was unwilling to make that choice. Cain wanted only the result he sought and when he didn't achieve it, he had nothing. Cain could not find solace in the fruits of his labor, because he did not choose to put God before himself. Cain thought he could "buy" God's grace, when in fact we have nothing God wants or needs other than a desire to know him.

Obsessed with Results

Unfortunately, we've become personally and professionally obsessed with results. We define our success by our stock options, our titles, and our net worth. We willingly sacrifice fulfillment for power and wealth. We allow ourselves to compartmentalize our lives to that end, to accept standards and practices of work that do not align with what we believe or know to be right, but are simply what someone has convinced us are the way to get ahead.

When we don't achieve our desired results of fame and fortune, we, like Cain, look to blame someone else. We see ourselves as victims of an unfair contest. We rationalize cheating, only to realize that there are no contestants. There are only winners and losers, and it's up to us to choose which we will be, not by the result we achieve, but by the purpose for which we decide to enter the contest.

In business we waste endless time and resources trying to dictate results, starting with the "end game" and working backward from there. Success, we've come to believe, is all about planning and control: Define the results you want to achieve and hold everyone's feet to the fire. Methodology becomes subordinate to process. Ethics get lost in the shadow of the bottom line.

Have you ever looked the other way at work and rationalized that it's just the way business operates, or that you don't have any power to change things? Do you try to do the right thing, or do you do what you think the boss expects, or what is most likely to get you a raise or a promotion? Do you ever get angry or jealous when someone else in your office gets attention or credit?

One of the more insidious byproducts of being results-oriented is that it allows us to rationalize any behavior. There were many people at WorldCom, it turns out, who knew of the false accounting that allowed the company to mislead investors. They rationalized their complicity by telling themselves that they couldn't do anything about the fraud or that they needed to keep their job in order to provide for their families. Some of them may now go to jail. None of them achieved the result they were seeking—on *any* front.

Like many business people who supervise others, I've had to eliminate jobs and terminate employees from time to time. Like most managers, I didn't enjoy it, but I convinced myself it was the "right" thing to do. I made the case to myself that if I didn't eliminate jobs, the company would not remain competitive and eventually everyone's job would be at risk.

That was true, as far as it went. The problem with that logic, though, is that it focuses on the wrong things—it focuses on the results. I was thinking in terms of cost and expense, jobs or no jobs. If I had been thinking about purpose instead, I might have found an alternative to letting people go. Perhaps I wouldn't have discovered an alternative, but as long as I believed the desired result dictated the action to take, my actions were guaranteed to be simplistic: cut expenses by eliminating jobs. It's a simple equation.

More to It Than Results

Have you ever noticed that some of the country's richest people never set out to be rich? They didn't turn down the money, mind you, but that's not what they focused on. Steve Jobs, the founder of Apple Computer, for example, says that in the early days of Apple the goal of the employees was "to put a dent in the universe." They weren't, in other words, focused on becoming a billion-dollar company or achieving a certain market share. They were focused on doing what was, in their mind at the time, the right thing.

What do you work for? Lifestyle? Bragging rights? God's grace? Do you ever make initial judgments about people based on their title, their friends, or their clothing? Do you ever think that just one more promotion or raise will make your job more fulfilling or your life more complete?

If you see your work simply as a means to an end, you're probably not getting much satisfaction out of it. If you define your goals in terms of title, authority, or income, you see the world much as Cain did. You believe it's the offering that matters, that the destination defines the path. In fact, as the Bible tells us, it's the other way around.

Business is commonly believed to be a brutal affair. Aggression, even ruthlessness, is frequently valued over character and faith. We are defined by what we accomplish, not by who we are or what we contribute. Competition, we falsely believe, is the route to victory, domination of the path to greatness.

It's become a badge of honor in business to be described as "results-oriented." It suggests you're serious about what you do and generally unsympathetic to excuses. You're no-nonsense. You know what you want and you find a way to make it happen.

In reality, though, *everyone* is results-oriented. Most people come to work each day wanting to do a good job and achieve the right results. Contrary to popular management theory, employees won't wander aimlessly or shun work if there isn't someone looking over their shoulder and telling them what to do.

What is the most common advice recruiters and outplacement experts give job-seekers these days? Talk about what you've achieved, not the jobs you've held. Potential employers want people who can get results, not people who contribute below the radar. Leadership, many executives wrongly believe, is all about achievement, not purpose.

It is, however, far more productive to hire good people without experience than bad people with experience. Cain may have been a great farmer, but ultimately *he* fell short, not his accomplishments. Abel, on the other hand, lost his life, but achieved eternal success by virtue of who he was, not by the flocks he had accumulated or the meats he offered.

In the early 1990s, I met a corporate chairman who was probably in his seventies at the time. He asked me how many employees worked for the company I was then the president of. I rather boastfully answered, "About five thousand." His reply took me by surprise. He said, "Oh, what a tremendous responsibility you have on your shoulders, being responsible for the welfare of five thousand families." You don't hear that kind of talk coming out of corporate America anymore.

Contrast that with the response given by Al Dunlap, former CEO of Scott Paper and Sunbeam, to a question put to him by interviewer Hedrick Smith concerning Dunlap's tough-guy image. Dunlap said, "Well, I think they know I'm a no-nonsense person. I'm not coming there to listen to all the excuses which they've been giving. That's what got them into trouble to begin with. I'm not there to hear what can't be done. I'm there to get results."

My first employer had the official strategy of achieving a 15 percent return on equity and 4 to 5 percent profit after taxes. That was it. Our CEO considered those goals to be a respectable performance standard, so that's what we told people our company was all about. We never really defined how or if we could do it. We'd find a way; that's management's job, or so we believed.

We seldom hit our target. It wasn't such a high bar relative to what other companies in other industries were doing at the time, but we were in a competitive, mature industry. And there was certainly no shortage of sincere effort. We fell short nonetheless.

Were we bad managers? Maybe. We were if you define good or bad on the one-dimensional basis of whether we achieved a pre-defined outcome. For a lot of people in business today, that is the case. It's a perspective—one that Cain could buy into.

Jack Welch, by contrast, says that his first appearance, as chairman of GE, before Wall Street's analysts was "a bomb." Welch writes, "It was, after all, my first public statement on where I wanted to take GE. You know, the vision thing. However, the analysts arrived that day expecting to hear the financial results and the successes achieved by the company during the year. . . . Over a twenty-minute speech, I gave them little of what they wanted and quickly launched into a qualitative discussion around my vision for the company. . . . As I moved into 'soft' issues like reality, quality, excellence, and (would you believe?) the 'human element,' I could tell I was losing them."

Compare that to the words written by Jeffrey Skilling and Kenneth Lay, the CEO and chairman, respectively, of Enron, in the Letter to Shareholders contained in the Enron Annual Report for the year 2000. They wrote, "Enron is laser-focused on earnings per share, and we expect to continue strong performance." Later in the letter they wrote, "Our performance and capabilities cannot be compared to a traditional energy peer group. Our results put us in the top tier of the world's corporations."

If you are the CEO of a public company in the United States today, it's tough not to be a slave to Wall Street, a world populated with number-junkies. Ironically, it was the investment world's preoccupation with results that lead to the mantra of "pay-for-performance" and the huge stock options that were ultimately justified by it. The reality is you'll lose your job if you don't give shareholders what they want. It's tough to convince your family and friends you've done a good job as CEO if your stock is off 90 percent and the board just dumped you.

Preoccupation with results is not a problem confined to the executive suite. It permeates entire organizations and leads to both personal frustration and weakened corporate performance.

Misguided Emphases on Budget and Performance Review

What are the two corporate processes that get the most time and attention in business today? The budget and the performance review. The modern excess in the importance attached to each is a product of our misguided belief that we can dictate results and that the methods will follow.

I'm not suggesting that budgets are not needed, but how often are budgets submitted only to be sent back for revision because they didn't deliver the "results" desired? Chances are it's never happened otherwise. It becomes a game. You pad the budget so that you have something to cut. Your boss forces you to cut it because he or she assumes you've padded it. You spend a few weeks going back and forth. Ultimately, you have a budget that may or may not be good for the company, but at least has finally been accepted.

It doesn't stop there, of course. You spend hours each week or month reviewing the actual results. It's not that you can do much about it after the fact. But you'll have to explain it to the boss so that he or she can explain it to his or her boss. And starting almost immediately you'll have to start submitting a revised budget, because even if the world in which you operate hasn't changed, some corporate executive has certainly changed his or her expectations.

For most corporations today, budgeting has taken on a life of its own. It absorbs huge amounts of time and effort with little incremental payback. It gets worse when you can least afford to waste resources—when times are tough. Whenever any company is laying off employees, you can bet that everybody left behind is spending a good part of his or her day crunching the numbers (i.e., defining the desired result).

Most companies' human resources practices are just a variation of the same theme. What the accounting department is to the management of assets, the human resource department has become to the management of people. Performance is all about "metrics." Pay and promotion turn on a statistical curve. Even your job is given a value and pigeonholed in the organizational matrix.

Once again, it's perfectly logical to ensure that employees know what is expected of them and how they have done against those expectations. But human resources today often goes beyond that in its attempt to fit in with the other disciplines and to support the results-defined goals of the corporation.

The Myth of the Market Share

One of those goals is likely to be market share. I have yet to see the strategic plan that didn't contain an exhaustive analysis of competitors and their market share. For some companies, it's a daily or weekly ritual.

I've never understood the importance attached to the concept of market share. It's just another result. Surely we must keep an eye on competitors, and changes in market share *may* shed some light on whether our ideas are working or our competition is about to run us into the ground. But an increase in market share is not *always* a good thing. What if it is not sustainable? What if we build a ton of expensive capacity only to find out that our additional market share was just an aberration? What if the sales department gave away the store to get it?

The problem is that results are just that—results. It's all scorekeeping. Success comes from doing the right thing again and again. It is the one thing you can control. If you do the right thing and get a good score, you've won on all fronts. If you do the right thing and get a bad score, you've still done the right thing and you've done all that you could. If you don't do the right thing, though, the score doesn't matter; you lose either way.

The Accountability Conundrum

Results are the father of accountability, which is perhaps the most abused concept in business today. It sounds so objective, so businesslike. Often, however, it reflects the height of arrogance. Business is a multifaceted process with a multitude of variables, many of which are beyond our control. To believe that we can control a corporation, a single business, a department, or even the results of one's own effort requires a belief in personal power that none of us have. In reality, we have only the power to act and think in the right way.

Years ago when I was a materials manager, our inventory had risen to much higher levels than we desired. I was called into a large meeting of senior executives, all sitting glum-faced around the immaculately-polished conference table in the board of directors meeting room. The CEO sat at the head of the table and demanded to know who was responsible for inventory. It was obvious from his tone that he considered the solution of our inventory problem to be as simple as defining the culprit and demanding accountability.

I explained that, at one level, *I* was responsible for inventory as materials manager. However, I went on to explain, inventory is analogous to the hub of the entire business process. Inventory levels are influenced by everything from the rate of sales to the production plan. In essence, I carefully explained to my CEO, *you* are responsible, if you insist on narrowing responsibility down to one individual.

My mistake, of course, was in assuming that accountability had anything to do with accuracy or fairness. Accountability has more to do with the authority to place blame and enforce penalties than it does with the objective identity of cause and effect.

Accountability is the executioner with a blade raised. It is a process of instilling fear and assigning blame. Both are necessary if you believe that people will do the right thing *only* in response to fear, and that doing the right thing won't always yield the desired result. I believe neither of those things because I don't believe there is any result that is *desirable* that is not respected by God.

Controlling Efforts, Not Results

In Genesis 4:6-7, "The Lord said to Cain, 'Why are you angry? Why is your face downcast? If you do what is right, will you not be accepted? But if you do not do what is right, sin is crouching at your door; it desires to have you, but you must master it."

A friend and business associate, now the chairman of a well-known and respected Japanese manufacturer, once said to me, "American business people always want to beat their plan by as much as possible. If they beat the plan by twenty or thirty percent, they are full of pride in what they believe is *their* accomplishment. This is not good. Unless you are a very bad planner, something unusual (i.e., out of your control) must have happened to allow you to beat your plan by that much. And because businesspeople always want to achieve better and better results, they will try to beat those results in the following year. But whatever was unusual will probably have passed, and they will begin to make poor decisions in pursuit of their unrealistic goal. They will fail *and* they will hurt the company."

If you have any responsibility for profit and loss today, there's no way you can or will go to your boss with a plan for the future that results in a reduced profit contribution. How many companies, in an otherwise strong economy, will guide Wall Street analysts to lower earnings projections for the coming year? Not many, and they won't do it more than once or twice. Every company says it will generate better results in the future. Every five-year plan—without exception—calls for the company to be bigger and more profitable at the end of the period.

What happens? Only a handful of companies will actually achieve their lofty plans. How can that be? How can so many management teams, many of which have enjoyed great success in the past, be unable to control their results in such a results-oriented environment? What is the difference between the winners and the losers?

The winners, of course, will imply that the difference is management. The losers will undoubtedly blame the economy, or at least some sequence of events beyond their control. But even the economy, as we define it, is just another result. Does it not seem logical that by being so preoccupied with results at the corporate level, companies contribute to the erratic performance of the economy as a whole?

If we can't always control results, what should be the focus of our personal and management efforts? Doing the right thing. And what is that? Thankfully, God has laid that out in black and white in the Bible. Come up with your own list if you must, but any variation from God's list will only put you back where you are. Believe me, I've tried.

Do you believe the world has changed? Do you believe business is more competitive today? Do you believe you have to play the game this way to get ahead? I don't. I believe these are just excuses to justify a doctrine of management and corporate behavior that is wrong *and* not working. Only when we accept, at every level of business, that doing the right thing is the key to getting the right result, will we consistently realize our true personal and corporate potential over the long term.

For Further Reflection

Do you consider yourself a results-oriented person?

What results are you working toward?

Do you ever let your actions or behavior at work conflict with what you believe to be right because you think you should or have to?

Whose acceptance do you seek?

How do you define success?

How do you judge your coworkers?

Have you ever done anything to a fellow worker out of revenge or a desire to gain relative favor in the eyes of the boss?

What does "doing the right thing" mean to you?

Where do you typically assign blame for your mistakes or problems?

Are you Cain or Abel?

Chapter 3.

Connectedness

One Body, Many Members

For by the grace given me I say to every one of you: Do not think of yourself more highly than you ought, but rather think of yourself with sober judgment, in accordance with the measure of faith God has given you. Just as each of us has one body with many members, and these members do not all have the same function, so in Christ we who are many form one body, and each member belongs to all the others. We have different gifts, according to the grace given us. If a man's gift is prophesying, let him use it in proportion to his faith. If it is serving, let him serve; if it is teaching, let him teach; if it is encouraging, let him encourage; if it is contributing to the needs of others, let him give generously; if it is leadership, let him govern diligently; it if is showing mercy, let him do it cheerfully (Romans 12:3-8).

In this passage from the New Testament, Paul begins to explain how we should live in recognition of God's boundless grace. He starts the selection by advocating humility and goes on to say, "Just as each of us has one body with many members, and these members do not all have the same function, so in Christ we who are many form one body, and each member belongs to all the others." Paul acknowledges that God has a different plan for each of us, but these plans are all connected and each is part of the others.

We Are Not Alone

Being connected to the world around us is crucial to our spirituality and our sense of self. If by our own arrogance we sever our connection with the people around us, conceit and self-promotion inevitably lead to emotional and intellectual myopia. If the connection is severed by circumstances, our self-confidence is eroded by our isolation and we wall ourselves into a cold, dark fortress of fear and anxiety. Either way, we become a prisoner of the status quo, stunting our personal growth and fulfillment.

We cannot achieve our full personal potential—the key to finding fulfillment—on our own. Realizing our full potential requires our personal effort and diligence, but cannot be achieved independent of the people and the world around us. We may not need their *help*, but we do need *them*. Sunshine, you see, does not come in single rays.

This is why belonging requires more than acceptance. It requires active involvement. We cannot be connected to others unless we reach out to them while being open to their reach. Growth requires a mutual embrace.

That is why perspective and attitude are only a starting point to real connectedness. We can be kind and caring and still not connected. As managers and supervisors, connection requires more than an open door and a willingness to listen to employees. Communication is not connectedness. Connectedness is an understanding and acceptance of Paul's statement that "each member *belongs* to all the others."

We can understand our place in God's creation only through one another. It is an understanding that is essential to our sense of purpose, the basis on which our lives acquire meaning. Without such understanding, there is no context to our lives, no basis for measuring our achievement.

Founded upon Giving

Strong's Exhaustive Concordance of the Bible cites more than two thousand uses of the the word *give*, or one of its variations, in the Bible. Christianity was founded on the idea of giving. God *gave* us his only son, so that we might be redeemed from sin. In Acts 20:35, we are told "It is more blessed to give than to receive." There can be no giving, however, without a willingness to receive. Giving and receiving are two sides of the same thing. One cannot exist without the other. Connectedness to the world around us requires equal amounts of both.

Learning to receive is one of the toughest hurdles many of us face in our spiritual growth. We are naturally uneasy with receiving because it requires a certain amount of abandonment. We must let our guard down and open the door to who we really are.

This is why connectedness is so important to our Christian faith and personal fulfillment. It is not enough to obey Christ. We must open our hearts to him. Only then can we truly follow Jesus. As I emphasized in chapter 1, faith is a choice, not blind obedience.

Without the willingness to surrender ourselves–to receive–it is impossible to be a true leader. All great leaders throughout history have been spiritually oriented. If our life-view is limited to our place in the corporate hierarchy or the prestige of our home address, the context in which we evaluate our work and our life is a relative one. We can never achieve fulfillment because there is always someone who has acquired more.

This is true at many levels. Corporate America's current crisis of confidence exists in part because corporate life is defined merely in terms of profits and stock prices. To say that a corporation exists to make money is like saying that a team in the National Football League exists to score points. Profits and points are important to each organization's respective success, but points are of little value if there are no fans, no connection between what the players do and what the spectators experience.

There is little or no connectedness between the owners, the management, the employees, and the customers of America's modern corporations. That's because our corporations operate in a spiritual vacuum. There is no context for their existence other than the price of their stock. A corporation has no purpose other than the promotion of its self-interest.

As a result, corporations today are distrusted, accountable to no one, and often callous and irresponsible toward employees and the communities in which they operate. We call it a crisis in corporate governance and morality, but it is a collective failure to connect the stakeholders of the corporation to each other and to the larger world in which they exist.

Connection, Performance, Competition

This lack of context and connection does more than undermine corporate credibility. It erodes corporate performance as well. In today's knowledge-based, customer-driven economy, every worker in every company must be a leader. Self-leadership is as important as group leadership to the performance of any business.

Leadership is all about choice and direction. What are my goals? How do I respond? How can I do better? These are questions every employee must answer each and every day. Just "doing your job" is no longer enough. These questions, however, require a larger context within which to be considered. Without purpose, we inevitably just go through the motions in our work and look elsewhere for our growth and development.

At the same time, no employee can realize his or her true potential without the ability to see his or her work in the context of a broader view of life. Simply making money is not enough. We need money to live as we have become accustomed to, but income without purpose is both illusory and hollow. It's like keeping score without knowing what the game is.

Unfortunately, companies today consciously and inadvertently disconnect their employees from the people and the world around them. There's a lot of talk about teamwork, but it's always in terms of "our" team versus the "opposing" team. Some companies even talk about family, but it is a family defined by corporate identity ("We are the Acme Company family"). The corporate idea of team and family, in other words, is exclusive; it implies a well-defined, "us/them" set of boundaries.

While such a culture may result in pride in the company and allegiance to its goals, it tends to isolate employees from the larger world. That isolation is reinforced by internal practices relating to job performance and promotion. It is hard to feel connected, for example, to those you are forced to compete with for recognition and advancement.

Contrary to a lot of current management thinking, competition is not the key to efficiency and productivity. Competition, in fact, is self-limiting. If competition is all that matters, performance standards are effectively established by the quality of the competition. The goal becomes to win the competition, not be the best we can possibly be.

Our business vernacular is filled with analogies to sport and war. I've used some here. In reality, however, business has little in common with either. Wars and athletic contests are digital events—there is a winner and a loser. Business, on the other hand, like life, is not a zero-sum game. Success in neither business nor life requires domination or defeat of someone else.

Faith and Tolerance in the Workplace

Employees are most disconnected, in the workplace, in regard to faith and spirituality. Most corporate employers openly insist that employees leave their religion at home. In the corporate version of "don't ask, don't tell," faith and spirituality aren't considered proper topics for the office or boardroom. Seldom are religious analogies invoked in company meetings, and few corporate speakers are invited to talk about God and profits.

It's a loss to both the employee and the company. From the employee's perspective, there's inevitable conflict. No religion supports character compartmentalization. Under no spiritual doctrine is it appropriate to have one set of values while working and another while at home. Faith is an aspect of life twenty-four hours a day, seven days a week.

The company also loses in many ways. First, of course, it has employees who feel compromised due to the lack of alignment between who they are and what they do. That has an obvious impact on motivation. Second, a non-faith-based employee management model inevitably breaks down into counter-productive turf wars, posturing, and office politics. And thirdly, the machinery of behavior modification and control that most corporations rely on to sustain a "competitive" corporate culture is very expensive. Few things in business sap the bottom line as greatly or consistently.

The biggest loss for both the company and the employee is the latter's inability to reach his full potential. As Paul explained, "we who are many form one body." We cannot fully realize our spirituality, in other words, isolated from each other. Knowing God is not a competition.

Instead of a workforce pulling the company along through realization of the full personal potential of its individual members, the company often becomes mired in petty and counter-productive squabbling. Contrary to the notion that competition motivates people to perform at their best, it often motivates them to devote time and attention to issues that have little to do with the company's success.

If you manage people, it's not enough that you are fair and tolerant. Walking the hallways, eating lunch in the employee cafeteria, and sending underlings an E-mail on their birthday, may make you nicer than most bosses, but it doesn't give you connection to your employees. Connection requires a sense of shared values and active mutual support.

Tolerance is one of the most misunderstood and abused concepts in society today. The need for tolerance is too often used to suggest that we cannot have a life-view. If "anything goes," there is nothing to share; there are no values on which to build connection. True tolerance requires acceptance of our differences without the sacrifice of our sense of purpose or our faith.

In the workplace, tolerance is often the justification for a values-blind work culture. There is a reluctance to articulate shared values out of fear of causing offense and the lawsuits that inevitably seem to follow these days. To have values, however, is not to be intolerant.

I talked with a small business owner about his desire to bridge his faith and his work. He told me that he had recently asked his employees to join him in prayer for a fellow worker who was seriously ill. The owner was obviously conflicted about his gesture. He did not want to force his faith onto his employees, but he genuinely felt that prayer was appropriate.

I believe it was a perfectly legitimate thing for the owner to do. He wasn't forcing anyone to participate. He was establishing *his* values, not forcing them on the organization, and this served as a starting point for greater connection.

Values and Company Culture

A values-blind workplace may appear to be free of conflict when in fact the conflicts are simply pushed out of sight. This obviously inhibits conflict resolution; conflicts simmer and eventually sap the organization's vitality and effectiveness. Even more importantly, the avoidance of values in the workplace precludes the kind of cultural environment that fosters real cooperation and naturally seems to elicit extra effort and commitment to the organization and its goals.

Talk to the original employees of a company that went from startup to industry giant about the company's success, and it is likely that they will talk about the original *culture* of the company. These high-energy cultures are inevitably defined by shared values and shared experiences. These employees typically recall that people reached out to one another. There was a true sense of family that created connection, and that connection gave purpose to the work.

Just as typically, if you ask these original employees what happened to that culture when the company became successful and grew larger, they'll tell you that the culture changed. Small teams became large organizations. Informality gave way to policies and procedures. Just pitching in was suffocated by job descriptions and performance reviews. In the paraphrased words of many, management—often new management—began to run the company like a "real business."

Doesn't that sound awful? It doesn't have to be that way. Business doesn't have to be a competitive event. Business exists for one simple reason—to create value for the customer. A successful company is one that provides a product or service that is worth more to the customer than it costs the company to produce or provide. The scorekeeping is all done in some common currency of monetary value, but value has no intrinsic monetary basis.

If you believe that the vast majority of people show up every morning wanting to do a good job, competitive motivation is of little value. It's a waste of time and effort to motivate a worker to be better than the worker next to him if he is already the best worker he can possibly be. Even more importantly, why motivate an employee to be slightly more productive than his peers when he has the skill to be twice as productive? Why measure employees against a standard that may not allow them to realize their full potential?

In fact, in an ironic twist of management obsession with efficiency, I believe most corporations are greatly inflating their costs through excessive controls and misguided attempts to program employee behavior and to motivate through competition. How much time do you spend in budget meetings? How many signatures does it take to authorize an expenditure that is a clear no-brainer? How many unnecessary E-mails do you get each day? Your answers to these questions have undoubtedly made my case.

So much of what is considered sound management today mirrors an innate distrust of people. Instead of providing employees with a door to the world around them, we confine them to their cubicles and tell them exactly how to behave. We talk about teamwork, but we promote self-serving competition that isolates employees and pits each against the others. It's little wonder that employees in this environment can hardly wait for the weekend.

"Company Policy"

Have you ever been told, "It's company policy"? Supporters of company policies will hide behind the need for consistency, and consistency can be a good thing. But it's not always necessary or appropriate. When a store clerk uses the company policy excuse, there is an immediate gulf between the clerk and the customer. All of a sudden there is an institutional barrier dividing them. Instead of allowing the clerk and customer to connect at some level to work out the problem, they're now separated by riot shields. The employee is made to feel like an ineffectual cog in the wheel and the customer is given one more reason to shop elsewhere.

An internal organizational disconnect can be just as damaging. Like most manufacturers, one of my former employers struggled with the issue of attendance. In a factory, attendance is a big deal because few people work in isolation. Companies go to great lengths to control absenteeism, often through elaborate policies. In our case, the company tracked "instances" of absenteeism or tardiness on an annual basis. It didn't matter one iota why you were late or absent; get too many instances in a certain period of time and a pre-defined penalty would be applied.

Supervisors loved the policy. Unlike fostering connectedness, which can take a fair amount of effort, it was easy to administer. The supervisor didn't have to sit down and talk with the employee and perhaps learn of a problem that was temporary or that the company could help the employee solve. Instead, the supervisor just made a few keystrokes in the computer and was done with it. When it came time to discipline an employee, the supervisor could shrug his shoulders and blame it on company policy.

Employees, not surprisingly, ultimately reacted in kind. In a variation of the old advice to be careful what you wish for, if the company wanted an institutional process, it's process that they would get. Every employee knew exactly how many instances he or she had and how far he or she could go before there would be any trouble. The company could rest assured that the policy pretty much set the minimum limit for how much tardiness and absenteeism there would be. And not surprisingly, there was a tremendous spike in absenteeism in the last weeks of the year, as people used up their "instances" before the slate was wiped clean.

Would the union go along with a less well-defined process? Of course not. At least not initially. Why should they? Unions are only playing the game that management has defined. At this point unions have a vested interest in the status quo. Nevertheless, most union officials I've worked with are genuinely interested in creating a better workplace and will be willing partners once there's a little connection and trust established.

Connection is the foundation of respect. Respect is strong where people share values, and values can't be shared without some medium for exchange and understanding. Without connection, there can be no leadership and the company is managed through authority alone.

Authority, even absolute authority, is not enough to run a successful business or department today. Having authority is like having the opportunity to hold water in your hands. No matter how tightly you exercise it, the water (i.e., productivity) leaks out. The day-to-day workplace is just too varied ever to establish rules and procedures for every possible situation. And even if you do get close, the cost of monitoring and enforcing compliance will quickly dwarf the cost of the product or service you provide.

Management effectiveness, in other words, is often suffocated by the machinery of management. Instead of putting so much effort into planning and control, into controlling behavior and promoting competition, management would be far better served creating an environment where employees feel a sense of common purpose and trust; where employees aren't forced to compartmentalize their faith but are encouraged to fit their work into the context of a sound life-view.

As business people, we are trained to think in terms of trade-offs. Trade-offs are the basis of competition: Someone wins, someone loses. What Christ has given us, however, is a world in which trade-offs are unnecessary. We can all know the glory of God. We don't have to choose giving or taking. We can be both givers and receivers in his kingdom. In fact, we *must* be both if we are to truly know him.

Connectedness erases the barriers and the gulfs that create trade-offs. If a company is connected to the world around it—is an active citizen in its community—and the employees are

connected to each other, everyone wins. Employees can realize their full potential, the company prospers from the work of
motivated, productive employees, and the community enjoys
the contribution of responsible corporate citizenship.

For Further Reflection

Is competition essential to business? Explain.

How could teamwork be improved at your company?

Do you consciously reach out to others? If not, why not?

Do you feel your work really represents who you are? Why or
why not?

Can you accomplish what you want to on your own? Explain.

Do you feel compelled to keep your personal values to yourself? Why or why not?

How can company policies be made more effective?

How could your company be a more active corporate citizen?

Do you feel connected to the world around you?

What is God's plan for *you*?

Chapter 4.

Leadership for the Common Good

A Joy and Not a Burden

Obey your leaders and submit to their authority. They keep watch over you as men who must give an account. Obey them so that their work will be a joy, not a burden, for that would be of no advantage to you (Hebrews 13:17).

This passage from the book of Hebrews affirms the importance of authority; at the same time, it suggests that authority is valid only when exercised for the good of all. Leaders, in other words, must be accountable to all they lead.

Most of my former bosses had a very different perception of authority, and chances are that yours does too. Many people forget that authority doesn't exist so that they can get promotions and earn more money. And it really doesn't exist so some people can tell others what to do. It exists, or should exist, solely for the purpose of promoting the common good.

Authority and Leadership

There is a big difference between authority and leadership. Authority is the *right* to do something. Leadership is the *opportunity* to have others follow your lead. When I was made president of the company I worked for, for example, the board of directors gave me authority to do certain things, such as sign contracts on the company's behalf, approve expenditures, and hire employees. They gave me only the opportunity to lead, however. *Being* a leader was up to me.

Legitimate authority, I believe, can be granted only by God. That doesn't mean God is going to hand you a scepter when you are put in charge of your department or company. It means that authority is legitimate only when it furthers God's plan. Thankfully, God is gracious and merciful, and there can be no higher good than that which he wishes for us.

Does that mean you should go into work tomorrow and disobey your agnostic boss because you don't think he or she is interested in furthering God's plan? Of course not. Authority is necessary to run any business. Decisions ultimately have to be made and it's not practical for everyone to participate in making all of them.

God has nothing against making widgets. As we learned in the story of Cain and Abel, however, it's not the widgets God cares about. God cares about us. If making widgets helps further his plan for us, God is surely all for it. If we use our authority to prevent others from furthering God's plan, however, we are abusing that authority. Ultimately, God will hold *us* accountable.

Parental Authority

A good example of the kind of authority that the writer of Hebrews was referring to is parental authority. It is granted by God to assist our children in developing in a way that allows them to understand and act upon God's plan for them. As every parent knows, if you're just looking for someone to mow the lawn or take out the garbage, it's a lot easier–and less expensive–to hire someone.

Children, of course, don't always want to acknowledge our parental authority. They may have a hard time, for example, understanding how our not letting them have another candy bar is in the common good. It is impossible for parents to rear a child without ever having that child question parental authority. The Letter to the Hebrews, teaches both children and parents that obedience must sometimes trump understanding.

Certainly I'm not suggesting we be abusive parents, or that we instruct our children to do things simply to enhance the relevance of the Letter to the Hebrews. I do believe, however, that God will hold us accountable for the job we do as parents and that being a good parent will inevitably cause our children to question our authority.

I believe that our inclination to challenge authority is a natural part of growing up. The best-case outcome is that children, when they become adults and acquire their own authority, will be inclined to think about authority in the way Hebrews lays out. God wants us to think about authority, just as he wants us to think about free will and choice—in reference to our relationship with him.

Corporate Authority

The most common abuse of authority I see in the corporate world is the exercise of unnecessary authority. All too often, authority becomes an issue of what we *can* do rather than what we *should* do. We flex our muscle simply because we have it. We distort authority into manipulative power.

I once had a vice president reporting to me who demanded that I provide him with two lists of names. On one he wanted the names of everyone in the organization who could tell him what to do. On the other, he wanted the names of all the people he could tell what to do. To his credit, he had the courage to articulate what just about everyone in every large corporation wants to know.

He blurred the line, however, between legitimate authority and power. To him, rank and title were all about control and discipline. It never occurred to him that he could legitimately tell people what to do—no matter where they were slotted on the organization chart—only if it ultimately served the common good.

Nearly every corporation utilizes some variation of the traditional organization pyramid—a Big Kahuna on top and cascading levels of diminishing authority on down from there. It's an organizational concept modeled after the military, with different titles and a few different protocols for enforcement.

It's an organizational structure that is ideally suited for coordination and control of large numbers of people. A military has to operate as a single, coordinated unit. Battles are generally won or lost on execution and the stakes couldn't be higher. If anyone fails to fulfill his or her role in the common effort, others may die. Authority, in other words, is in *everyone's* interest.

The military may seem to equate authority and power. There's a reason for that. Soldiers in battle have to do things that are counterintuitive, even contrary to their natural instinct for survival. And they have to do them quickly, without hesitation. Blind obedience, in other words, is for the common good and it requires discipline and programmed behavior. Following orders has to be second nature. That's where drill sergeants come in. They may seem abusive, and sometimes they may well be, but they ultimately serve the common good.

Business had management needs similar to the military's—with obviously lower stakes—back in the beginning of the twentieth century. More and more work was being done in large, sprawling factories and most people were only one or two steps removed from the actual production of something. It was a production-based economy and the coordination and control of that production and the logistics that supported it pretty much determined a company's success or failure. Productivity reigned supreme among the variables of financial health.

Today, by contrast, most companies live or die by innovation. Good execution is still very important, but it's often not enough. Because of easier access to capital, the global availability of capable contract production, and the migration of production-technology development from in-house engineering departments to independent third-party specialists, the barriers to entry have been significantly lowered in most industries. New products are commoditized almost overnight and competitive differentiation on the basis of manufacturing excellence is extremely difficult to achieve and maintain.

As a result, most work today is knowledge-based, and companies must continually develop new knowledge in order to stay ahead. Since non-manufacturing-based competitive differentiation is often easy to imitate, new avenues of differentiation must be continually developed. Effective leadership today, in other words, demands more inspiration than assignation.

Communication is still important, but the nature of the communication has been turned on its head. Replacing the need to keep a large organization moving in disciplined lockstep is the need for a constant flow of new ideas reflecting the evolving needs of the marketplace. In other words, it's more important to be responsive than disciplined, although discipline obviously can't be cast aside.

Responsiveness, of course, requires getting close to the action. Since getting close to the action does little good if you can't do anything about it, most management experts today agree that responsibility and decision-making should be pushed as far down the organizational pyramid as possible. Getting close to the customer is the new mantra of management gurus.

Few companies, however, have been very successful at it. While the failure is often blamed on issues of attitude and motivation, the real problem is not desire, but opportunity. Famed college football coach Lou Holtz once said, "The difference between winners and losers is *not* that they want to win. Everybody wants to win. The difference is what they do when they get knocked down." People at lower levels of an organization often know what needs to be done in order to respond to change; they simply aren't given real chances to put their knowledge into action.

Most corporate attempts at pushing ideation and problem-solving down into the organization have involved some form of cross-functional team. They almost always fall short. Shortly after the T-shirts are handed out, the acronym finalized, and the banners hung, the members become either sidetracked or frustrated. The team gets off into an area it can't influence, or it gets bogged down trying to acquire the necessary cooperation.

Even getting employees within a single department to take greater ownership of problems and to be more active in identifying opportunities has been frustratingly difficult for most companies. Employee empowerment, as such initiatives are often labeled, has seldom produced much more than good copy for the company's annual report to shareholders and the employee newsletter.

The reason is simple: All of these initiatives have been undertaken within a traditional corporate model of authority that often fails to differentiate between authority and power. Everybody still has a boss who will largely define job security, eligibility for promotion, and compensation. People react to what that boss inspects, or oversees, not what her or she expects. The boss can't delegate authority while retaining power. As long as someone else is in control of the employee's future, he or she will resist ownership of the boss's problems.

Distortions of Authority

The distorting power of authority can be very subtle, even unintended. I once had a boss who considered himself a consensus-builder. No label could have been further from the truth. Once he made up his mind about something, he would visit each of his direct-reports individually, ostensibly to solicit our opinions. Before we could offer our opinions, however, he invariably told us what he thought and why. When it finally came our turn to talk, it was obvious he was really there to get only your agreement, not your input.

Consensus-building in corporate America today is more often than not an authoritarian dictate dressed up as employee involvement. It's a charade that can do great damage. It is a great irony of modern corporate life that while there is so much talk about the flat organization, servant leadership, the importance of team-building, and the need for employee initiative, authority has actually become more concentrated and more self-serving. Despite all the rhetoric about risk-taking, management is more than ever focused on preservation. And despite all of the buzz about accountability, authority often gets channeled into abusive power.

Authority isn't a bad thing per se. At many levels, it's absolutely necessary. Without it, companies would collapse in chaos. While the concept of authority isn't the problem, however, the way in which corporate authority is currently exercised surely is. My first boss used to remind me, "This isn't a democracy." Or he would dismiss my opinion with, "You're not entitled to an opinion; you're still wet behind the ears." When things didn't work out, however, *he* always took the heat. I never felt as if my job were on the line over a single opinion. I felt free to learn and grow to my full potential. His rhetoric or manner aside, he was a leader inclined to use his authority for the common good.

Abuse of Authority

Abuse of authority is nothing new in corporate America. Ruthless, overbearing corporate titans have always been among us. Several developments in business, however, some of them not particularly obvious, enhance the risk of abuse today and reinforce the need for new forms of diligence and protection. Seniority and experience are no longer the defining criteria of selection for advancement that they once were. While that has invigorated younger workers (it gave me the chance to run a corporate division at the age of thirty-two) and helped to keep perspectives fresh, it has also resulted in executives with little or no experience, even in the company or department they lead. They have no history and no expectation of an extended future to temper their actions.

There's a good reason that twenty-somethings do not run the Pacific Fleet or command NATO forces. The military obviously requires youth, and many young people are given extraordinary responsibility. There is recognition, however, that experience is essential to defining how and when that responsibility is to be exercised.

Once again, the marginalization of experience can have benefits, particularly if change ceases to be linear—that is, if things stop evolving along a relatively continuous path. If the future looks nothing like the past at any level, what good is experience? It may be a hindrance. As we saw in the early days of the personal computer and the Internet, technology has the potential to change the paradigm. When that happens, openness to the new paradigm may be more important to leadership than having experience with a now-outdated paradigm.

In a similar vein, before the initial public offering, or IPO, became every businessperson's dream, there were far fewer publicly owned companies. Only the biggest and most proven companies were listed. Day-trading wasn't a profession for the average American. And while management was empathetic to investors, executives generally weren't slaves to Wall Street.

On balance, management kept its eye on a more distant horizon than is often the case today. Executives tended to retire from the company with which they had spent their entire career, and few were dumped in the flash of a press release. Legacy was a powerful motivator. Corporate executives were as sensitive to their reputations as to their financial track record.

In part, this broader focus simply reflected the social standards of the time. Whether you define those changes as an enhancement of tolerance or a decline in moral values, there were simply more natural constraints on behavior and a broader view of achievement. Life was less of a free-for-all and more of a choreographed production.

That was undoubtedly influenced by the fact that people were physically and mentally less isolated. Executives were more likely to live in the community, among the people they managed, instead of in a secure, gated community or in some distant city a corporate jet ride away. If you fired someone, there was a good chance his son delivered your newspaper or his daughter watched your kids when you and your wife went out. In short, people generally had roots in their work that they don't have today.

For all of these reasons, the reality of corporate America today is that the people in charge do not *"keep watch over you as men who must give an account"*–at least not in the sense the passage from Hebrews expresses. As long as they don't break any laws or violate any SEC regulations, and as long as they deliver results, no one is likely to challenge how well the flock has been watched over.

Layoffs and terminations are quickly announced at the first signs of a down quarter. Executive compensation is off the charts while the people who actually do the work are fighting to keep what they have. Little effort is devoted to employee fulfillment beyond that which will contribute directly to the bottom line. And few companies play any active role in the communities in which their employees reside, beyond paying taxes and providing jobs.

All of this is rationalized, of course, as a simple reflection of current competitive realities. There's little empirical evidence, however, to support the implication that being less accountable to employees or less responsible corporate citizens is the key to corporate success. In fact, it's been pretty well documented that no company has ever saved itself into long-term prosperity. Corporate restructurings and rationalizations, in and of themselves, are not effective turnaround strategies.

Reforming Authority

There need to be major reforms in how we run America's corporations and in the purposes they serve. We must recognize that legitimate authority exists only for the common good. The authority exercised by our corporate leaders is no exception. They must be held accountable for more than the price of their stock.

There are also some very sound, practical business reasons for such reform. The most powerful is the fact that no one, not even our CEOs, our vice presidents, or our department supervisors, can escape their past. We all see what we expect to see, and what we expect to see is inevitably shaped by our prior experience. Executives like Bill Gates, Steve Jobs, and Michael Dell will be as captive to their past experience as all of the grey-haired executives who failed to see the opportunities these men saw in their youth.

There's a very good reason, in other words, for keeping corporate authority in check. We are all one-trick ponies. We can't help it—as human beings, we are naturally limited. Once again, if change is linear—the future is just an extension of the past—that's no problem. Change frequently is not linear, however, particularly where technology is involved. It's the reason we see extremely effective executives go on to new assignments and fail. They don't stop trying or simply lose their competence in their sleep one night. They move into a world that is very different from the one in which they developed their perspective.

Obsolescence of perspective is particularly problematic when it involves the CEO. When companies were traveling along fairly predictable paths, when their technology and their markets changed at a methodical pace and in predictable ways, the biggest challenge facing the board of directors was to insure that the CEO didn't screw up. The board, in fact, would have been shocked and incredulous if the CEO recommended "re-inventing" the company or fundamentally altering the business model.

Today, by contrast, the board is often looking for the CEO to do just that. It is one of the reasons the board frequently goes outside the company today to find a CEO. And it's one of the reasons that CEOs are often allowed to run large public companies as if they own them. The board and the shareholders are looking for a CEO with a "personal vision." They want a CEO who can personally "shake things up." The CEO has become the "Chief Enlightened Officer," that one individual who is, by implication, singularly able to see the future and determine how the company should react to it.

This has created a celebrity class of CEOs who are the voice and face of their companies. They are given extraordinary power to redefine companies they did not create and may know little about. While many of these CEO celebrities have ultimately lost their jobs, that typically doesn't happen until the damage is already done. The fact that these CEOs were ultimately asked to leave doesn't so much show that all CEOs are ultimately accountable as it shows the imprudence of putting so much power in the hands of one person to begin with.

Somebody clearly has to be in charge. Their authority, however, should be no greater than it absolutely has to be for the company to function. There should be checks and balances in place, not just at the top, but throughout the organization—

all the way down to the lowest-level supervisor. Most importantly, all authority should be exercised *only* for the common good. It's not just the word of God; it's good business.

For Further Reflection

How is authority defined at your company?

Who do you believe you are accountable to?

Do you sincerely listen to those of greater experience than you?

Why does God tell us to follow our leaders?

Have you ever been told to do something you were uncomfortable with? How did you react?

What makes a great leader?

What leadership skills do you need to work on?

What are the elements of the common good?

How can your company further the common good?

How will you be remembered by those you lead?

Chapter 5.

The Importance
of Perspective

The Parable of the Sower

That same day Jesus went out of the house and sat by the lake. Such large crowds gathered around him that he got into a boat and sat in it, while all the people stood on the shore. Then he told them many things in parables, saying: "A farmer went out to sow his seed. As he was scattering the seed, some fell along the path, and the birds came and ate it up. Some fell on rocky places, where it did not have much soil. It sprang up quickly, because the soil was shallow. But when the sun came up, the plants were scorched, and they withered because they had no root. Other seed fell among thorns, which grew up and choked the plants. Still other seed fell on good soil, where it produced a crop—a hundred, sixty or thirty times what was sown. He who has ears, let him hear."

. . . "Listen then to what the parable of the sower means: When anyone hears the message about the kingdom and does not understand it, the evil one comes and snatches away what was sown in his heart. This is the seed sown along the path. The one who received the seed that fell on rocky places is the man who hears the word and at once receives it with joy. But since he has no root, he lasts only a short time. When trouble or persecution comes because of the word, he quickly falls away. The one who received the seed that fell among the thorns is the man who hears the word, but the worries of this life and the deceitfulness of wealth choke it, making it unfruitful. But the one who received the seed that fell on good soil is the man who hears the word and understands it. He produces a crop, yielding a hundred, sixty or thirty times what was sown" (Matthew 13:1-8; 18-23).

Jesus uses the parable of the sower to explain the importance of perspective. Some listeners hear the word of God but are quickly snatched away by evil; others receive it and are joyful, but the belief is only superficial and eventually evaporates in the heat of life; yet others hear the message but are led astray by wealth or power. Those who hear and understand the message of Jesus, however, prosper and flourish, like seeds planted in the richest soil.

At the most important level, Jesus is delivering a message about faith. Not all who claim to have faith—not even all who believe they have it—really do. And some who do will be overcome by the difficulties and/or temptations of life. It's a message Jesus delivers to both the audience and to the disciples, cautioning the latter, I believe, not to be fooled by outward appearances and to be cautious of over-confidence or declarations of premature victory in their efforts to spread the word of God.

Perspective and Motivation

At a personal and business level, the parable of the sower speaks to our personal motivation. If I want something, why do I want it? Do I desire it for reasons consistent with my faith, or do I have an ulterior motive? Is temptation manipulating my logic or does my reasoning grow from fertile ground?

In the business world, personal ambition is openly admired and encouraged. To be labeled a "go-getter" or a "hustler" is to receive one of the highest compliments in business today. You don't get promoted unless you display outward enthusiasm and a strong desire to get ahead. The company values employees who will work hard and do "whatever it takes."

But what if "whatever it takes" involves falsifying records or cheating customers? There's a difference between a healthy desire to be successful and blind ambition. On the surface, they may look similar. Below the surface, however, the difference in motivation amounts to a difference in life-purpose.

We've all read in recent years about the corporate executives who cheated investors out of billions of dollars. Most of these executives didn't need the money. What they needed was a healthy perspective on right and wrong. In many cases, no one was more surprised at the transgressions of these men than their closest friends. Some were even considered men of faith, but their faith, as the parable goes, was planted on the rocks of envy and greed.

Dishonesty doesn't come in doses, however. Honesty is digital—an act is either honest or dishonest. There is no in-between. If you are cheating someone, it doesn't make it all right if that person deserves it or can overcome it. The cheating says something about the soil in which the faith of the one who cheats is planted.

My uncle managed a large department store. I recall a conversation in our kitchen many years ago in which my father asked him if the store had a problem with employee theft. My uncle said it did. My father then asked if it was the young employees who were at the root of the problem, as he was obviously inclined to assume. My uncle replied, "No, the older employees who have been there a long time are typically responsible. They believe they've earned it—that the store owes them something." That's exactly, I'm sure, how the corporate perpetrators led off in handcuffs in recent years felt at the time of their malfeasance.

Do you believe it's all right to splice a few more televisions into your cable line without telling the cable company? Do you download pirated music onto your computer? It doesn't really matter that the cable company has a monopoly or provides poor customer service, or that the music companies have contributed to the country's moral decay. What they are is fairly obvious. What are you?

Out of Control

One of the most common excuses we use to justify actions that we know to be wrong is our lack of control. "I can't do anything about it anyway" is our frequent explanation for giving in to temptation or not taking steps to do what we know to be the right thing.

There is no greater contributor to personal stress than the sense that we are not in control. A factory worker can be under far greater stress than a CEO. An air traffic controller can be less stressed-out than an office assistant. Each of us is equipped to deal with pressure. We are inevitably overwhelmed, however, by situations that are beyond our ability to manage.

Many things in life and business are beyond our control. There is one thing, however, that we can always control—our will. We can always make the right decision for the right reasons no matter how little impact that may have on the larger situation. Only we determine whether our faith resides in fertile soil or among the rocks.

There are, of course, always consequences to our decisions. Every decision—even the decision to do nothing—is a choice. And the most debilitating choice of all is the choice to surrender our will, our control over self.

When we forfeit our choice, however limited its impact may be, we inevitably feel guilt. Guilt is an emotion of failure, of missed opportunity to do what we know is right. Guilt is why we can never avoid choice. If we choose, we may have to live with consequences we don't like. If we don't choose, we will inevitably drown in the dark waters of guilt and regret.

Jesus is not telling us, in the parable of the sower, that making the right choices in life will shield us from pain and suffering. He is saying that making the right choices will sustain us in times of hardship. Even crops planted in fertile soil may suffer flood or drought. No matter what happens, however, the soil remains fertile. By making the right decisions we will find everlasting spiritual peace.

How the Good Guys Win

I find the parable of the sower to be relevant at many levels in business. The first is my heartfelt conviction that the "good guys" always win in the end. It may take a long time, but character and integrity always triumph over deceit and trickery, even in business.

I've always believed that a free marketplace is ultimately an honest marketplace. If you have a segment of business that is exceptionally profitable, you can assume that it won't last. I don't care what the product or market is or how hard you work to maintain the status quo—you won't. The marketplace will not let you. I've seen it time and time again. Companies assume that a highly profitable product line or business segment will always remain that way, so they don't prepare for the inevitable day when it no longer does.

The same holds true for people. One of the messages Jesus delivers through this parable is that the inner self is ultimately exposed. Again, it may seem as if the process takes forever. You may watch for years as the most undeserving and reprehensible people in your organization get all the recognition and rewards that you know they don't deserve. Their day will come. I've yet to see the exception.

The parable of the sower demonstrates that goodness ultimately prevails. Perhaps the greatest business lesson we can discern from the parable has to do with the value of a loyal customer base. Customer loyalty is the most important variable in all of business. If you can retain your customers, you will succeed nine times out of ten. If you can't retain your customers, on the other hand, you will ultimately fail no matter how many new customers you are able to add in the meantime.

It is always more expensive to gain new customers than it is to keep current customers happy. It is a truth that crushed many of the dotcom startups. They wrongly believed that if they built it, to paraphrase the movie *Field of Dreams,* customers would come. They didn't. They never do. As discussed in chapter 1, customers have to be motivated, and motivating potential customers is an expensive proposition, especially early in a company's life.

What is the key to customer retention? Motivation obviously plays a role. Once a relationship is established, however, retention is not so much a question of motivating customers to buy from you as it is of raising the bar high enough that your competitors cannot motivate your customers to switch. It is also a matter of avoiding a bad experience that motivates customers to stay home and do without.

Keeping customers from switching will break the bank, however, without customer loyalty. Consider what's happening among the big Detroit automakers. They are all trying to prevent customers from switching brands by matching the rich financial incentives offered by the competition. Everyone suffers. Even if they are successful in holding their market share, they have paid a steep price in profitability and financial health.

Contrast their plight with the Japanese and German automakers that generally enjoy stronger customer loyalty and have been less reliant on financial incentives to retain customers. Even with steep financial incentives, the American automobile manufacturers have generally not been successful in taking customers away from these more profitable manufacturers.

What is the basis of customer loyalty? Certainly quality and service play a role. There's little question that a poor purchase or ownership experience will cause customers to look elsewhere and that it will be very difficult and expensive to get them back. Few companies are successful over the long term with poor quality.

Built on Values

Sam Walton, the founder of Wal-Mart, built his retail empire on a very simple formula. More than any other retailer in the world, he was committed to efficiency in getting merchandise to his stores and on the shelves. Efficiency allowed him to offer lower prices and still make a profit. It also gave him a leg up in keeping merchandise in stock and the opportunity to deal fairly and openly with his suppliers. Coupled with his commitment to motivated employees and a friendly store environment, it was a formula that rocketed Wal-Mart to success.

I believe there's something more fundamental to Wal-Mart's success, however, and I believe it is the secret to customer loyalty. It is the institutional honesty that you find in a company that is not afraid to have values. It is why, in part, despite the simplicity of their strategy and the openness that they've always had about sharing the secret to their success, no one has been able to duplicate Wal-Mart's formula.

Sam Walton, from everything I've read and heard, was an honest man who felt a great sense of connection with the people who worked for him and the people that shopped at his stores. By all accounts, even once he became a billionaire, he lived his life pretty much as he always had. He drove a red pickup truck and ate breakfast at the local diner he had been going to for years. He was what he was, he was comfortable with that, and people could tell.

Walton had a strong set of values, and he wasn't ashamed of them. His values are evident in everything Wal-Mart stands for and does, from everyday low pricing (honesty) to the greeters at the door (friendliness) to the apparent willingness to give people a chance to work who might not get that chance elsewhere (community). Most importantly, you get the overwhelming sense that all of it is genuine. Sure, these things are all part of Wal-Mart's marketing strategy. There's nothing wrong with that. The important thing is that their marketing is honest and sincere.

That's where a lot of companies fall short. One of the reasons Kmart was forced to file the largest retail bankruptcy in history, in my opinion, is that the people who ran the company at the time did not shop at their own stores, and, more importantly, looked down upon the people who did. People can smell arrogance the way a dog smells fear. You can't hide it away in the executive tower; whiffs of it are going to get through to the people you want to be your customers.

Some of the strongest brand names in American history were built on very specific values that the company successfully communicated in everything they did. Coca-Cola, for example, was obviously proud of its southern American values, no matter where in the world they were trying to sell their products. Kodak promoted a clean, family image that honestly reflected their strong commitment to their employees and to the community in which they were headquartered. Even the famous quip of Charles E. Wilson, president of General Motors during the late 1940s, that "What's good for General Motors is good for the country," was honestly portraying the strong American values of his day. It may seem like an arrogant statement in today's social climate, but I have no doubt it resonated with GM's customers when he said it.

The Real Power of Brands

Marketing observers have noted with some alarm that there has been a noticeable decline in customer loyalty in recent decades. It's frequently referred to as a decline in the power of brands. It's a trend almost always blamed on a more fickle consumer. I don't buy it, however. I don't believe today's consumer is fundamentally different from the consumer of the past.

The decline is certainly not the result of less advertising. American advertisers spent $237 billion in 2002, according to *Advertising Age* magazine, trying to get you and me to buy their products and services. The consumer is literally drowning in corporate communication.

What's really changed, I believe, is summarized best by the very fact that corporate America views the decline in customer loyalty as an issue of brand to begin with. The problem is not that brands have lost their value to consumers; it's that brands are no longer built on values.

Marketing has certainly become slicker in recent decades. Some would argue that it's more scientific. Everything is now tested in focus groups, and companies are endlessly researching the marketplace for signs of what will work and what won't. Companies still work hard to establish an image—called "positioning" in today's jargon—but that image is invariably linked to an emotion or some superficial form of status. Companies want to be seen as "hip" or "rebellious" or "sexy." What they don't want to stand for, however, is a specific set of personal values.

As a result, however, we have created a sea of faceless, valueless institutions that consumers can't identify with. Consumers know what various brands claim to be able to say about the customer, such as "I'm fashionable" or "I'm successful"; but consumers don't know about the company and its purpose, and how that relates to them and their life-purpose. Consumers are thereby not motivated to remain loyal to a particular company—instead they make choices based on the fashion or whim of the moment and not on solid values.

Making Connection

As I indicated in chapter 3, connectedness, which is critical to customer loyalty, turns on shared values, not shared identity. We evaluate commitment not just on what the other person or company can do for us, but what we want to do for them. Do I want to give this retailer another chance even though the coffeemaker I purchased last week had to be returned? Do I really want to buy this brand of children's clothes, even though I can buy this other brand for half the price? Will I change car brands for zero percent financing or a bigger rebate?

We all want to be connected and we connect to the people and the institutions that reach out to us and that share our values. The parable of the sower goes both ways—the quality of a relationship is directly proportional to the quality of both parties to that relationship. A business will not establish a bond with the consumer if that business cannot convince that consumer of its honesty, its ethics, and its purpose beyond profits and the price of its stock.

This is why the crisis in corporate governance that began with the collapse of Enron is an issue that all businesses must face. It is true, in my experience, that most businesses are not run as Enron was. That doesn't matter. All of corporate America has lost credibility and it won't regain it until people believe that corporations have a purpose beyond making executives rich, and corporations, even though they are institutions, can't have purpose unless they are willing to stand for certain values.

Purpose will not take root in business until there is a sense of connectedness throughout the organization. It won't be dictated into existence. There must be a sincere sense of mutual commitment among all employees and respect for the customer. All employees have to think not in terms of what they can take *from* the customer, but what they can do *for* him or her.

That's unlikely to happen until the company accepts values in the workplace. The values-neutral workplace is inhospitable to connectedness. We connect to each other—and to God, as I'll discuss in the next chapter—through a shared perspective on the values that define who we are.

For Further Reflection

Do you ever feel entitled to be dishonest? Do you believe there is such a thing as harmless dishonesty?

What does your company stand for? Is it sincere? Explain.

How do you *really* feel about your customers?

Think of two or three companies that you like to do business with. What values do you associate with them? Are they values you share?

Do you feel in control at work? At home?

Do you believe companies should have a greater purpose than making money? Why or why not? If so, what should that purpose be?

Do you ever avoid making decisions? Why or why not?

Are you really the person you describe yourself as? Explain.

What are the thorns and rocky places that threaten you?

List the values that would characterize a company named after you.

Chapter 6.

The Burden
of Process

The Beatitudes

Now when he saw the crowds, he went up on a mountainside and sat down. His disciples came to him, and he began to teach them, saying:
"Blessed are the poor in spirit,
for theirs is the kingdom of heaven.
Blessed are those who mourn,
for they will be comforted.
Blessed are the meek,
for they will inherit the earth.
Blessed are those who hunger and thirst for
righteousness,
for they will be filled.
Blessed are the merciful,
for they will be shown mercy.
Blessed are the pure in heart,
for they will see God.
Blessed are the peacemakers,
for they will be called sons of God.
Blessed are those who are persecuted because of
righteousness,
for theirs is the kingdom of heaven.
Blessed are you when people insult you, persecute you and falsely say all kinds of evil against you because of me. Rejoice

and be glad, because great is your reward in heaven, for in the same way they persecuted the prophets who were before you" (Matthew 5:1-12).

In the Beatitudes, Jesus both identifies the personal qualities each of us should strive for and reassures us that our perseverance in pursuing these qualities will be rewarded. Each of these qualities can often best be described by noting characteristics *lacked* by those who embody these qualities. The poor in spirit are *not* over-confident; those who mourn are *not* vengeful; those who are meek are *not* arrogant; those who seek righteousness are *not* self-centered; those who are merciful are *not* judgmental; the pure in heart are *not* consumed with greed or lust; the peacemakers are *not* consumed with conquest; and those who persevere are *not* swayed by popular opinion.

These qualities also represent a state of being rather than a form of action. Not one of them says, "Go for it!" or "Make it happen!" or "Crush the competition!" or any of a long list of behaviors that business frequently promotes. Nowhere in the Beatitudes, in fact, are we told to be aggressive, even though aggressiveness is often the most prized quality for an employee to possess in the eyes of his employer.

Aggression is at the core of what has been taught in business for the last twenty years. We think of business as a process of out-muscling the competition, breaking down its defenses, and overrunning its position. Our image of victory is the business person standing with his foot on the carcass of his competitor, sword raised in triumph.

Thankfully, the rhetoric of aggression seems to be losing some of its hard edge in the post-9/11, post-Enron world. Nonetheless, if there's a common theme to nearly all of the management theory taught today, it is that business people must be proactive, they must "make something happen," in the words of many management gurus. We're advised to research our customers, manage by walking around, plan, follow up, re-invent, break what's not broken, and so on. In short, we're advised to go on the offensive.

There's nothing wrong with that—to a point. As I argued in a previous chapter, if you simply build it, they (customers) will not necessarily come. Even if interest in your product or service is sparked by word of mouth, that word of mouth has to be ignited somehow. To borrow an analogy from the world of physics, the customer's natural state is to be at rest.

Sometimes, however, businesses are so obsessed with being proactive that they spend far more time and effort pursuing an action than it will ultimately be worth, even if it is successful. Companies can also become so focused on "carrying out the plan" that they overlook an opportunity that just happens along. In both cases, companies are victims of the processes they've developed for managing business.

The Process Trap

Making things happen requires a process of definition and execution, planning and control. These processes take time and money and can impede our ability to see things as they really are. Often they take on a life of their own, and we start to view new realities as they relate to our process instead of seeing these new realities in their proper context.

Processes naturally develop a "self-maintaining" momentum in an organization. That's understandable. Processes typically involve people, and people rightly develop a stake in their job. The purpose for their work, and the continuing need of their services, are frequently perceived to be riding more on the process than on the original reason behind the existence of the process. In today's business climate this is often more than a perception—it is the reality.

For this reason, once a process is in place it can be extremely difficult to stop or re-direct. Anything can be rationalized, even financially. Accounting, as we've now all learned, is far from an exact science. Numbers are merely representations, and what they represent is frequently far from clear or precise.

I knew a CEO who, when the company was doing well, decided that the company should buy its own jet. The CEO loved airplanes and it was obvious to everyone that he really enjoyed having this plane. He could cite all of its specifications from memory. He even kept a model of it on the credenza behind his desk, right next to the portrait of his family. He was a very good businessman, too, so he wasn't inclined to be frivolous. Each year he personally asked the chief accountant to do an analysis of the plane to make sure that it could be financially justified.

The chief accountant was a smart businessman, too. He knew that no corporate jet could really be financially justified. You probably won't agree with that assessment if you're accustomed to riding on one, but it is the truth. That doesn't mean that a company shouldn't have a corporate jet. It does mean that having one is not saving the company any money.

The chief accountant and his assistants spent hours determining how much each passenger-trip on the corporate plane would have cost on a commercial airline. That, by itself, is not an easy task, since it depends on how far ahead the ticket might have been purchased, among other factors. The real unknown, however, was exactly how many of those passenger-trips were really necessary. It's easy to justify going places if you have a corporate jet to do it on. Not surprisingly, executives frequently asked where the plane was scheduled to go and made their travel plans accordingly.

In the end, the annual analysis always showed that while the case was not a strong one, the plane *probably* could be justified if you were willing to take some liberties with the assumptions. The CEO, I'm sure, read it carefully, shared it with the board, and filed it away just in case any shareholder or employee should question the prudence of the company owning the plane.

The analysis wasn't fraudulent, mind you. The chief accountant didn't make up numbers or fudge the results. He knew what the desired result was, however, and he didn't think this was a big enough issue to fight the CEO on. He saved his political trump cards for even more serious company matters.

The point is that the process of analyzing the financial wisdom of owning the jet was a complete waste of time. The accounting staff could have devoted the time they spent on this process to do something that was really going to save the company money or bring in new business. It was the sort of charade that gets played every day in the business world.

In a similar vein, most large companies have a very formal process for approving new customer credit and monitoring ongoing credit balances. Credit management is a cornerstone of modern financial management and most companies wouldn't dream of cutting corners, for good reason. As one credit manager is fond of saying, "It's only a gift until the customer pays for it."

Nonetheless, when it comes to process, most companies take a one-size-fits-all approach. At many companies, it doesn't matter whether the customer needs $10 of credit or $100,000 of credit, the process of review is the same. As a self-employed person, I know from experience. The paperwork for establishing a line of credit is frequently too much trouble—I don't even keep records of some of the numbers that are sometimes asked for. Instead of dealing with all of the paperwork, I frequently just find a way to do without or to accomplish my objective in some other way or with some other company.

As Bob Hope once quipped, "A bank is a place that will lend you money if you can prove that you don't need it." We've all shared the experience. Sometimes the process of doing business with a company just isn't worth the trouble the customer has to endure. This is particularly true, I've found, where there is a division of responsibility within the company and the people who are trying to get your business and the people who must approve it have no shared incentive. The employees who give approval often become known as the "sales prevention" department, not because they're bad people or don't have the company's best interests at heart, but because their personal stake is in the process, not the outcome.

I like the approach to credit management that a colleague once told me his father used. When my colleague graduated from a very prestigious business school, he offered to look over his father's business to see if anything he had learned would be of benefit to his father. His father was extremely successful, but it was good practice for the son and was of no risk or burden to the father.

In reviewing his father's business practices, the son was stunned to learn that the father never did a credit check on new customers and never monitored the credit performance of existing customers. When he confronted his father with this gross dereliction, his father chuckled and said, "That would take my time away from my good customers. God will take care of the ones who don't pay me."

The man's business was very successful, so who are we to argue with his logic? While his credit practices will sound like the height of naiveté to a lot of business executives, they were probably the right ones for him. If he had spent a lot of time managing credit, he might not have had the time to do all of the things that made his business successful.

The problem with processes like credit management is that they aren't as precise as they appear to be. Some of the biggest and most sophisticated companies in the country still get hit with sizeable credit losses from time to time. They might be worse off without a formal credit management process, but the dividing line between how much process is justified and how much is wasted time and effort is frequently a very blurred one. Of course, that's not what the people who manage the process will tell you.

Process or Common Sense?

One of my favorite stories involving business process run amuck involves an internationally known consumer products company. I won't mention the name because it really could have been any company and my point has to do with process, not the company itself. The story involves a promotion the company ran some years back in its European division. It was a variation of a broad category of promotions often referred to as "gift-with-purchase." Only in this case, the gift was worth far more than the purchase.

I first became aware of it while browsing at a department store in London. I was riding the escalator to an upper floor and couldn't help but notice the sign at the top of the escalator announcing the promotion. The sign said that if you buy this product, at a cost of £95, or approximately $160 at the time, you would receive a free round-trip airplane ticket to the United States. Knowing that the ticket was worth much more than £95, I walked away scratching my head, puzzling over how the company could possible justify such a promotion.

At dinner that night, I asked a British colleague if he was aware of the promotion and wondered if he had any insight into the logic behind it. He immediately let out a hearty laugh and explained that the promotion was a mistake and that the company responsible was the butt of many jokes around the corporate offices of England. The company, my colleague had heard, was not legally able to withdraw the promotion once it started, and was projected to lose many millions of English pounds before it was all over.

I have no inside information as to what happened, but there's little doubt in my mind that the company was a victim of process. I'm sure that the promotion was put to rigorous financial analysis. That requires making an assumption regarding how many of the gift-with-purchase coupons will actually get redeemed. The promoter often makes little or no money on those sales where the coupon is actually redeemed, but, *on average*, only a small percentage of coupons, usually less than 5 percent, are actually redeemed. While a lot of customers may be persuaded to make the purchase because of the coupon, many of those frequently forget about the coupon or simply decide redemption isn't worth the effort.

My guess is that the redemption rate assumption used came from the company's own records or from some very reputable consulting or industry trade group. It was undoubtedly based on a huge pool of data from numerous "similar" promotions. It was, by implication, accepted by business professionals who were, I suspect, very bright and very well educated.

Clearly, this promotional idea was never put to the "common sense test." If anyone had stood back from the process of financial analysis and looked at this promotional idea as a consumer, it should have been obvious that the redemption rate for the free trans-Atlantic plane ticket would be extremely high and that, in fact, there are a lot more people interested in air travel than there are interested in this particular product. Many of them will—and did—buy the product just to get the coupon.

Nowhere can process do a company more damage, however, than in the area of product development. I don't know how Henry Ford came up with the idea for the Model T, but I'm sure it didn't come from a focus group. (Focus groups were not used until after World War II.) The Ford Motor Company did have extensive market research to support the Edsel, however. Unlike the Model T, the Edsel was a flop and the name is now synonymous with new product blunder.

Four decades later, a change-driven new CEO would decide that Ford's use of focus groups and quantitative market research wasn't providing enough product distinction. He sent small teams of designers and engineers out for eight weeks of "customer immersion," a practice that led Ford's product development chief to go club-hopping in London with a group of young people until four o'clock in the morning.

The new product development team, however, came up with the 2002 Ford Thunderbird, a remake of the 1950s classic. Said division president Jim O'Connor at the time of the launch, "This car, its style, the statement it makes, the feelings it evokes, all will make it an icon in its own right." It was to do for the Ford brand, executives believed, what the Viper did for Dodge.

The company planned to make only 25,000 Thunderbirds a year, in line with the product's exclusive positioning, a hefty price tag, and the limited market for two-seat sports cars. Just over 19,000 were sold in 2002, however, and sales through March, 2003 were down 21 percent from the prior year. The company has now announced that it will stop producing the car after the 2005 or 2006 model year.

Ford, of course, is not alone in introducing new products that just don't live up to expectations despite a rigorous "modern" new product development process. In the 1960s DuPont lost $1 billion over seven years trying to sell its imitation leather, Corfam, to a marketplace that just wouldn't buy it despite some of the most sophisticated marketing in all of business at the time.

In a much smaller arena, when I became the president of a consumer products division, I tried to introduce more customer input into the product development process by setting up a committee of company sales people. Prior to that, product development had been largely the prerogative of the design department and senior management. We weren't large enough to afford a lot of market research, so I thought the salespeople were in the best position to know what was going on in the field.

I personally spent a great deal of time working with this committee. In the end, however, I garnered more frustration than insight. It invariably seemed that the committee would recommend that the company simply produce a version of our competitor's most recent successful product—at a much lower price, of course. We didn't need a committee for that!

Am I suggesting that businesses should anoint a "guru" of product development and allow him or her to make decisions unchallenged? No. And that's an emphatic no. I am suggesting, however, that it's easy to over-think the new product development process. More importantly, it's easy to overspend on the *process* of new product development.

A lot of companies are enamored with focus groups. The idea is to put "normal" consumers around a conference table and ask them questions or get their response to product samples or ideas. There's usually a facilitator who runs the meeting, but the sponsoring company's marketing personnel sit behind a wall that allows them to see the participants but not vice versa.

Focus groups are expensive and, in my experience, generally ineffective. The participants are being paid to have a reaction, so they usually do. Whether or not that reaction is in any way indicative of their reaction as a consumer is anybody's guess. It's a process that sounds prudent—who can argue against getting the input of potential customers? But it is of little benefit relative to its cost in practice.

I sit on the board of directors of a company that makes gutters. That's right, the things that collect rainwater from your roof. It's a wonderful company and I thoroughly enjoy my involvement. Sometimes, however, I believe that the executives there are too close to their product. I understand how that happens. Their livelihood, after all, depends on gutters. But when an executive starts waxing eloquent about the newest gutter accessory the company has developed, and how excited customers are going to be when it's available—a claim supported by market research—I often want to shout, "It's only a gutter!"

Product is why companies exist in the first place, and new products cost a great deal of time and money to develop, so it's understandable that companies want to choose wisely when they decide to go ahead with the development of a new product. If the company gets it wrong, it is sure to be a drain on the company's earnings and may open the door for a competitor to take customers away. Nonetheless, the cost and the risk need to be kept in perspective.

Process and People-Management

Companies have a different challenge when it comes to managing employees. There are lots of laws and regulations to satisfy. Sometimes there's a union contract to abide by. And every employer wants happy, motivated employees who are committed to the company's success.

This makes the human resource department a breeding ground for process. There's a specific process for hiring people. There's another process for evaluating performance. And there are endless processes for enhancing morale and promoting productivity. Almost all of them are a waste of time and money.

I have a good friend who is a former teacher. She became a stay-at-home mom, but her kids are grown up now and her husband travels a lot as a sales executive with a large corporation. She therefore decided to take a part-time job working at a retail gift store that is part of a national chain.

My wife and I were having dinner with this couple one night and the woman began to tell us about a seminar she had attended at work. It was attended by all of the sales associates, including the part-timers. They were being paid their normal hourly wage, so no one was particularly upset by the idea of just sitting in a chair for an hour or two.

The seminar was conducted by an outside consultant and the topic, according to my friend, was determining the "color" of your personality. The objective was to increase sales, but the connection between increasing sales and personality color was never made clear. My friend thought the seminar was not only a waste of money, but in fact made the company appear rather idiotic to its employees. "If they really want to increase sales," she said, "they should take the money they're spending on this consultant and put another salesperson on the floor during busy periods."

Why is it that companies so frequently seem to lack common sense? The short answer is the corporate propensity to establish processes. And ineffective, costly processes that are already established in the work flow tend to propagate even more of the same.

In the case of the personality-color seminar, I'll bet the real culprit is the annual performance review or the process for handing out promotions, bonuses, and wage increases. Somebody back at headquarters, in other words, is trying to make a name for himself, to stand out from his colleagues, so that he can turn these processes to his advantage.

He knows that simply suggesting that more salespeople be added won't get anyone's attention as an innovative idea and may earn him a reputation with superiors for not being financially responsible. He has to come up with an idea that is out of the ordinary, that may deliver superior results, and will be difficult to objectively measure for success. A personality-color seminar is perfect. It sounds innovative and cutting-edge, has surely never been done before, and will be next to impossible to evaluate.

I don't mean to suggest that all of this happens at a conscious level. I suspect that the employee behind the seminar sincerely believed it was an excellent investment. But that's the problem with process; it quietly inspires irrational behavior. The people involved just don't see it coming.

A lot of corporate nonsense simply boils down to the fact that business people like to feel they are in control when in fact they are not. Can you imagine the HR director admitting that there really is no accurate way to measure employee performance or that the hiring process is really a crap shoot? Can you imagine the sales manager going to his boss and explaining last quarter's fabulous sales with a shrug of his shoulders? Of course you can't.

In a study that is sure not to be taken seriously in any boardroom in America, Northeastern University psychology professor Judith Hall found that just about everybody can be the boss and is comfortable in a leadership role. It shoots a gaping hole in the myriad processes companies use to evaluate job performance and assign authority.

Nearly all business processes, when taken to an extreme, are a waste of time and money. It is nice to believe that we can actually define a desired result and then make it happen by way of a process, but in reality we can't. That doesn't mean our efforts have no effect. It just means that our process-centered actions are a lot less effective than we like to admit.

Once again, business is no more or less complicated than life itself. Business isn't a self-contained realm. It is a voluntary part of our existence. Everything we need to make the most of that existence, to be all that we can be and to achieve everlasting life at God's side, was provided by Jesus in these eight beautifully simple Beatitudes. Hire people that live by them and your business will prosper like never before.

For Further Reflection

What personal qualities are encouraged at your company?

Do you try to be aggressive in your job? Explain.

Does your company keep its processes in check? Choose one company process and analyze it.

What, if any, of your personal processes have taken on a life of their own?

Do you believe that you can make anything happen if you just work on it hard enough? Why or why not?

Are you expected to control anything in your job that really isn't in your control? Explain.

Which of the Beatitudes best describes you?

Why does God admire the qualities described by the Beatitudes?

Does the management of your company admire these qualities?

Which quality do you most want to be known for?

Chapter 7.

Putting Experience to Work

Balaam's Donkey

Balaam got up in the morning, saddled his donkey and went with the princes of Moab. But God was very angry when he went, and the angel of the Lord stood in the road to oppose him. Balaam was riding on his donkey, and his two servants were with him. When the donkey saw the angel of the Lord standing in the road with a drawn sword in his hand, she turned off the road into a field. Balaam beat her to get her back on the road.

Then the angel of the Lord stood in a narrow path between two vineyards with walls on both sides. When the donkey saw the angel of the Lord, she pressed close to the wall, crushing Balaam's foot against it. So he beat her again.

Then the angel of the Lord moved on ahead and stood in a narrow place where there was no room to turn, either to the right or to the left. When the donkey saw the angel of the Lord, she lay down under Balaam, and he was angry and beat her with his staff. Then the Lord opened the donkey's mouth, and she said to Balaam, "What have I done to you to make you beat me these three times?"

Balaam answered the donkey, "You have made a fool of me! If I had a sword in my hand, I would kill you right now."

The donkey said to Balaam, "Am I not your own donkey, which you have always ridden, to this day? Have I been in the habit of doing this to you?"

"No," he said.

Then the Lord opened Balaam's eyes, and he saw the angel of the Lord standing in the road with his sword drawn. So he bowed low and fell facedown.

The angel of the Lord asked him, "Why have you beaten your donkey these three times? I have come here to oppose you because your path is a reckless one before me. The donkey saw me and turned away from me these three times. If she had not turned away, I would certainly have killed you by now, but I would have spared her" (Numbers 22:21-33).

We all see what we allow ourselves to see. Objectivity is largely the reality we are willing to accept. In this case, both Balaam and his donkey were looking at the same thing, but only the donkey was open to the angel's presence. As a result, Balaam reacted in a way that was inappropriate in the actual circumstances.

In chapter 6, I noted that the qualities described by Jesus in the Beatitudes all involved a lack of something. Living as God wishes, in other words, is as much about what you don't do as it is about what you do. Qualities such as humility are qualities of absence, not action.

Similarly, Balaam is a man of action—a man accustomed to getting his own way. His immediate reaction to the donkey's behavior is not to wonder what the donkey sees that Balaam does not, but to become enraged with what he believes is the donkey's insubordination. His error is in taking action when being receptive to the donkey's perspective would be the more appropriate reaction.

At another level, this is also a story about experience. As the donkey points out to Balaam, the donkey's past behavior gives Balaam no reason to believe that the donkey is simply disobeying him out of laziness or disrespect. Balaam fails to give weight to that experience in deciding what to do. He simply assumes he knows the reason for the donkey's behavior.

The Cost of Little Experience

When, at the age of thirty-two, I was put in charge of a company with more than $100 million in sales, I didn't put much stock in experience either. I scoffed at any suggestion that I should be cautious due to my lack of experience. A decade later, however, although the company had been very successful over the prior ten years, I had to wonder what the board of directors had been thinking when they made me the boss with so little time in the saddle.

At the start of my career, the people in charge almost always had grey hair. It was very rare for anyone to attain the title of vice president before the age of forty. In the lingo of the day, you had to pay your dues before you would even be considered for executive management.

That all started to change, of course, when twenty-something college dropouts started building companies that took leadership of the information technology revolution. Youth was suddenly hot in corporate America. Experience was no longer an asset. It was a liability. The world had changed, or so it was believed, and experience in the old world was considered a barrier to understanding this new one.

Ironically, if we had thought about Balaam's donkey, we might have realized that our assumptions about change were unfounded. Throughout the course of history, every generation has believed that its world is changing more rapidly and more fundamentally than the world of its parents. Experience, if we had consulted it, would have reminded us that change is a historical constant.

At the time I was a division head, the vice president of marketing was a man with more than thirty years experience. He was very enthusiastic and supportive. Once a decision was made, he was behind it 110 percent even if he had argued against it. Nonetheless, I came to view his experience as a real anchor to the company's marketing innovation. It seemed that every time someone had an apparently fresh idea, this executive would point out that it had been tried before and failed.

At one point I became so frustrated by what I considered to be his unwillingness to accept new ideas that I blurted out, "You know what your problem is? You've got too much experience." I was a firm believer in the old adage that the people who actually accomplish things first are the ones who aren't aware that it can't be done.

To his credit, however, he gave me new insight into experience. He said, "I don't bring up history because I don't think we should do it. A lot of great marketing ideas failed initially because of poor timing. The fact that something failed ten years ago doesn't mean we shouldn't try it today. But if we are going to go ahead with it, let's at least be aware of what happened the last time around."

That's probably one of the best explanations of how to use experience that I've ever heard. Experience is at the same time both a great advantage and a potential anchor for progress. Balaam, after all, had plenty of experience with his donkey. He ignored it, as he found out, at his peril.

Even when something dramatically new comes along, a closer look often reveals a familiar pattern beneath the surface. A friend of mine was one of the first two dozen or so employees of Lucasfilm, the creator of the Star Wars movies. At dinner one night we were talking about writing—he was a screenwriter as well as a special effects modeler—and he pointed out that there were only five or six different stories ever told by all of the films ever made. The idea behind Star Wars, he said, was no more than "a wagon train in space." Originality came in the execution.

The Truth about Change

A donkey isn't the fastest of God's creatures, nor the most pleasing to the eye. It is, however, a surefooted animal that is not prone to acts of irrational spontaneity—like leaping over the edge of a cliff. That makes it the perfect fit for some jobs. The problem is that it can be a little stubborn and it's sometimes hard to know, as Balaam discovered, when it's being surefooted and when it's just being set in its ways.

Of all the animals, I would say the donkey provides the best analogy for understanding success in business. More often than not, the plodder will prevail in business over the one who is fleet. That's because, in part, change never actually occurs as quickly as it appears to be occurring. But the plodder also prevails because perseverance in the face of inevitable failure—as my marketing colleague taught me—is the most important ingredient of business success.

One of the reasons change seems to sweep through like an unexpected puff of wind is that we don't see it until it hits and catches our attention. It is the phenomenon behind the difference in the common observations that grass "grows," while a flower "blossoms." You go out in the garden one day and a beautiful flower catches your eye, giving the impression that it came to life very quickly. In fact, the flower has been growing continuously, just as the grass around it has.

The Internet has been heralded as nothing short of revolutionary. When it first burst onto the popular scene in the 1990s, it was predicted that it would change the way we live and work nearly overnight. It has had a big impact in a very short period of time, to be sure. But the Internet has already celebrated its thirtieth birthday. It had been around for two decades before most of us had any idea what a Web site or an E-mail was.

Similarly, the ATM machine, which most of us consider a modern-day, indispensable convenience, has been around for nearly half a century. The first bank ATM was introduced in this country in the 1960s, and the bank executives at what was then Chemical Bank, the first U.S. bank to install an ATM, were very skeptical that customers would actually use it. In fact, customers wouldn't warm up to it for a couple of decades.

Most people, I suspect, believe that the Internet and the ATM machine are relatively new inventions that caught on like wildfire. They aren't and they didn't. We have the impression of dramatic, swift change because most of us were not aware of either until their use had grown to the point that we couldn't help but notice.

In addition to evolving more slowly than commonly believed, the businesses that are most closely associated with the change they bring about are often not spontaneously visualized by their creators, but more or less stumbled upon. The person who started the company had some experience in a related company or knew someone who had an idea but didn't see its potential. For example, it might be reasonably argued that IBM, not Bill Gates, started Microsoft. IBM was developing a personal computer at the time and wanted to license an operating system to run it. Whoever got the business was sure to be a huge success. Bill Gates saw the opportunity, jumped in, and Microsoft was born. Who knows where Microsoft would be today, however, if IBM hadn't entered the personal computer market or had decided to program the operating system internally.

The Track Record Trap

Most great entrepreneurs have a string of failures to go along with their successes. Even Thomas Edison, the holder of 1,093 patents for different inventions, formed the Edison Portland Cement Company to produce everything from cement houses to concrete pianos. The famed inventor of the light bulb and the phonograph, in other words, was as fallible as any other business person.

It is a huge mistake to assume that a person's track record will be the best indicator of his or her future performance. In assessing employees' future potential, it is less important to assess what they have done than it is to assess what they have learned and how enthusiastic they are about trying again. You can rest assured that the person who has made no mistakes in the past will eventually make one—perhaps a whopper. The person who *has* made mistakes in the past, on the other hand, will eventually get it right if he or she is willing to learn from them and plow on.

Unfortunately, most businesses today evaluate, reward, and promote employees almost entirely on the basis of their record. As a result, many employees who ultimately have great ideas are stuck at the bottom of an organization, where they can do little to turn their ideas into reality, and many fast-trackers zoom to the top just in time to fail miserably.

My father's family lived in northern New Hampshire, not far from the base of Mt. Washington, so my siblings and I were destined to become skiers. Like all beginning skiers, I fell a lot. I had difficulty accepting that part of the sport. When I fell, I felt embarrassed, as if I had failed in some way. My father, however, always consoled me by pointing out that if you're falling, you're learning. "The people who never fall are never going to get any better than they are," he would say.

I believe that's true about life in general and certainly true about business. Those who have never failed are unlikely to have achieved much. For a career or a business to be among the best, chances must be taken along the way.

It used to be that companies promoted people based largely on how long they had been on the job. Today, of course, businesses want to "raise the bar" of performance and mistakenly believe that the best way to do that is to advance everyone on the basis of ability.

That assumes, however, that ability can be measured or observed. I submit it cannot be measured, at least not accurately enough to serve as the basis of something as important as who the leaders of your company are going to be. What someone has done in the past is not a proxy for what he or she will contribute in the future. A track record is only that– a record of what they've done.

When I was in the silverware business, our biggest retail customers were department stores. The buyers responsible for our product category were typically in their twenties, in their first buying assignment, and fully expecting to be promoted or to leave within a year. "Buying tabletop," you see, carries little prestige within department stores because it is a relatively small category. The status categories are apparel and cosmetics. That's where all the senior executives come from because that's where you get noticed.

As a result of this desire, coupled with the fact that the stores prided themselves on the theoretically "enlightened" business practice of promoting people strictly on ability, the tabletop buyers weren't content to do the right thing for the business and its shareholders. They wanted to make a huge splash, get noticed, get promoted, and leave someone else to deal with the mess when it all came crashing down. It happened time and time again.

This scenario repeats itself throughout all of business on a daily basis. If your company is committed to advancing and rewarding people based on ability alone, that probably means that you will be judged not just on your record, but on how your record compares to the record of the those you are competing with for recognition. To borrow another sports analogy, that means you've got to hit the ball out of the park. A string of singles will not get you the recognition you need to stand out in the crowd. You have to swing for the fence, because that's how you get noticed and remembered.

What does that mean for the company? It means constant change, whether it's necessary or not. It means a lot of people are striking out when they could be hitting singles or doubles and setting the company up to score. It means people are motivated to take risks for the wrong reasons. "Break the mold" becomes "bet the farm" in the hope that they will have some dramatic immediate success and get noticed by the people who determine who gets rewarded and promoted. The result is customer-depriving, bank-breaking chaos. Sure, a few people will end up with something impressive for their annual performance review, but the overall performance of the company is likely to suffer.

Forced change is the reason that every company eventually hits a rough patch in the road. Business people can't help themselves. If the business is doing well, they'll buy another company or add a new product line that will drain all the cash from the original business. If a business slows down for a reason outside the control of the company, executives will make changes anyway, often making matters worse or delaying the recovery that would have followed when the cause of the original problem went away.

When was the last time you heard a business executive at a successful company say that the company wouldn't be trying anything new because it didn't want to mess up a good thing? It doesn't happen, because we falsely believe that the primary function of management is to change things. To paraphrase a noted business consultant's advice to business, "If it ain't broke, break it."

Turnaround consultants get paid a lot of money to bail out sinking companies. It's very hard work, but the formula for getting a company back on its feet is pretty simple. The cure typically involves identifying at what point in its history the company was doing well and reversing the key management decisions that have occurred since then. Chances are that there is still a very profitable business in there somewhere that is being dragged down by all the "great" new ideas that management has had over the years.

There is not one stitch of empirical evidence to prove that promoting people on their record is any more beneficial to the company than promoting them based on seniority or any other criterion. That's not to suggest that record should be ignored. Ideally, people should be promoted on a combination of experience, character, ability to learn, and enthusiasm. Other than experience, however, these are difficult attributes to assess and quantify. As a practical matter, therefore, there should be no single formula for assigning promotions and raises, but a qualitative approach that considers all of these things.

Uninformed Change

A corollary to the theorem that basing advancement on achievement inevitably leads to unnecessary, costly change, is that everything in business is the way it is for a reason. It's a truth worth repeating: Whatever a department or business does, no matter how nonsensical it may now seem, it is done that way for a reason. The reason may no longer be relevant, but we should know that reason before we start changing things.

I believe uninformed change has cost American business billions and billions of dollars over the last two decades. It's a problem that has been greatly accelerated by the total disregard for experience and the related propensity to hire senior executives from outside the company and even outside the industry. These outsiders know exactly why they're there. They are there to bring change—to be "change agents," in the jargon of the day—and bring change they do, often with disastrous results.

How do I know? I've done it. Like a lot of young people in business today, I started my career with an unhealthy arrogance toward the past. That something had been done a certain way for as long as anyone could remember was, in my mind, the best reason for changing it. I didn't care to know the history of the practice; I thought I knew better. In many cases, the company paid dearly for my arrogance.

Thankfully, I started my career at a time when mistakes were acceptable. I never feared for my job. I knew I wouldn't be a vice president in five years, but I also knew that a few well-intentioned mistakes weren't going to derail my career. Likewise, my boss knew I wasn't going to steal his job and he encouraged me to take chances. In fact, I believe he gave me the permission to proceed with a few projects that he knew wouldn't work just so I could learn from the experience.

Fear and Accountability

That probably wouldn't happen today. Executives aren't just competing with their peers for the next promotion; they're competing with the recent college graduate in accounting who wants to take their job away. They know that mistakes will not be tolerated. If it's a big enough mistake, one that the boss might lose *his* job over, you'll be out on the street before you can even figure out what went wrong.

It's called accountability, but I believe it is one of the biggest barriers to corporate performance today. People have to take risks to get ahead (the "track record" thing), but they know that if they make a mistake they'll be gone. So what do they do? They play politics—they posture, they betray, they do whatever it takes to take credit for the successes and pass off the blame for the failures. Don't believe for a moment that this is not what happens at your company.

Fear, the power behind accountability, is a poor motivator. Sure, it gets the adrenaline pumping, but to what purpose? Fear causes you to destroy or to flee whatever it is you fear, not to understand it or work through it. There are times when fear is necessary, but a constant diet of fear will cripple an organization in the long term.

Drawing on Real Experience

Another corollary of the achievement falsehood is that companies today frequently disregard the knowledge that retiring employees are taking with them. More often than not, the employees left behind are more intent on laying claim to the retiree's office and furniture than on assimilating the knowledge and experience he or she is taking away.

We were having a problem with our silverplating process one August and the engineers just couldn't figure out what was causing the problem. Silverplating, for the layman like me, involves dipping the product in different vats of chemicals in which metals like silver are suspended. The vats are then charged with electrical current, causing the suspended metal to cling to the product. It takes a lot of fairly sophisticated chemical engineering, and my employer had the best chemical engineers in the business working on the problem.

Thankfully, someone was smart enough to contact the recent retiree who had run that particular plating line and ask him if he had any advice on how to solve the problem. It turned out that he was very familiar with the problem. Some years ago, he told the engineers, the operators and engineers at the time ran into problems about this time every year and they finally traced the problem back to the water. The water used came from a municipal reservoir which is typically at its lowest point during the summer months. As a result, something about the water changed, playing havoc with the delicately balanced plating process.

When asked what they did to solve the problem, the retiree said they dumped a bag of raw potatoes into the plating vat and the problem went away. The engineers, of course, were incredulous. None of them had ever associated potatoes with silverplating before. They tried it, though, and sure enough, it worked.

Why hadn't the retiree told anybody about this before he left? My guess is that nobody asked him. As the retiree himself said, he didn't know who had come up with the idea or why it worked; he had just been doing it for years. Perhaps he did tell someone and that person dismissed it as a ridiculous relic of a less scientific past.

Similarly, when I resigned as president and a director of one company to become the CEO of another, not a single director called me to ask if there was anything he should know. One or two called to congratulate me and wish me luck, but no one made the effort to ask if there was anything about the situation that hadn't been put on the table. They didn't, in other words, put any value in my personal experience. They assumed they knew better.

Granted, departing employees often have an axe to grind. (I didn't.) You can always sort that out. Why not at least hear what they have to say, on the off chance that they will say something of great surprise to you? What have you got to lose? If you choose not to ask, you take the chance that what you don't learn will hurt you more in the long run.

Balaam's donkey was saving Balaam's life. Yet Balaam admits that he would have killed the donkey if a sword had been handy. It's a lesson each of us can learn from. Be careful of what you think you know. Be conscious of what you don't know. Value experience. It's amazing what we can learn from a donkey if we simply listen.

For Further Reflection

In what way is experience respected at your company?

What assumptions have you made about someone else's behavior, only to find out that those assumptions were in error?

Do you believe there is more change today than in the past? Why or why not?

Do you believe personal performance can be measured? How?

Would you put your employer's interests above your own? Explain.

Do the right people get promoted at your company? Explain.

What does your past say about your future? Is your past an accurate indication of the future?

Are you allowed to make mistakes in your job? Do you allow others to make mistakes?

Do you believe in changing things just to "shake things up"?

Are your eyes open?

Chapter 8.

Following Your Own Lead

A Tree and Its Fruit

Watch out for false prophets. They come to you in sheep's clothing, but inwardly they are ferocious wolves. By their fruit you will recognize them. Do people pick grapes from thornbushes, or figs from thistles? Likewise every good tree bears good fruit, but a bad tree bears bad fruit. A good tree cannot bear bad fruit, and a bad tree cannot bear good fruit. Every tree that does not bear good fruit is cut down and thrown into the fire. Thus, by their fruit you will recognize them.

"Not everyone who says to me, 'Lord, Lord,' will enter the kingdom of heaven, but only he who does the will of my Father who is in heaven. Many will say to me on that day, 'Lord, Lord, did we not prophesy in your name, and in your name drive out demons and perform many miracles?' Then I will tell them plainly, 'I never knew you. Away from me, you evildoers!'" (Matthew 7:15-23).

The truth always comes out. Did your mother ever tell you that? It applies to character as well. If you don't get ahead on your own hard work and merit, yours will be a false success and it will bring you no satisfaction or pleasure. Similarly, if a business is not built on creating legitimate value for the customer, it will ultimately collapse under the weight of its trickery and deceit.

Trust

In 2003, the Federal Trade Commission (FTC) began accepting registrations for a national do-not-call list. Telemarketers will be forced to take registered phone numbers off their contact lists or face substantial fines. The FTC expects registration of up to sixty million phone numbers in the first year alone, nearly one-fifth of all the residential and cell phone numbers in the United States.

The telemarketing industry is apoplectic, predicting that the new restrictions will cause it to lose up to $50 billion in sales annually. If true, that works out to approximately $500 in lost sales for every household in America. What does that tell you about how much consumers really want or need these products and services?

The telemarketing industry has become as big as it has for one reason—it works. As much as we may not be able to stand these unsolicited sales pitches, companies wouldn't be calling unless the technique was effective and profitable. Whether we like to admit it or not, most of us are still susceptible to the smooth sales pitch.

A former boss of mine told me a story about just how susceptible we are to a good pitch. When he was in college, he spent one summer selling, door-to-door, some kind of furnace attachment. I don't recall exactly what the furnace attachment did, but it was fairly expensive.

One day, one of the salespeople who had been selling these attachments for a while made a bet with my boss and another college kid. He said, "You two guys go down each side of this street and sell as many attachments as you can. I'll go down after you and I bet I will sell more attachments than both of you." They took the bet and, of course, the old pro won. The veteran salesman knocked on the doors of houses that the rookies had just visited, and actually turned many a "no" into a "yes."

That doesn't mean that he was a fraud or a cheat. In fact, many of the most successful direct marketers sell some of the best quality products in their category. What he knew, though, was that his high quality product itself was not enough. He needed to present in a way that inspired trust and confidence if he wanted to successfully close the sale.

My mother once bought a vacuum cleaner from a door-to-door salesman. She did a lot of vacuuming and had worn out more than a few machines. This vacuum had a new innovation. It created suction by swirling water into a whirlpool and catching the dirt in the water instead of in a bag. It worked well, as the salesman demonstrated, and was a lot easier and neater to clean out. I don't recall the price, but I remember my father was incredulous when she told him how much she had spent. Nonetheless, my mother had that vacuum until she sold the family home some thirty years later, still raving about how well it picked up dirt.

My wife and I don't vacuum as much as my mother used to, but we have owned our share of vacuums. Our current vacuum was purchased from a direct marketing company as well, and I have to admit that I was getting a little annoyed with this company at the time for all of the advertisements they were running. The spokesperson, who owns the company that shares his name, is just a little too enthusiastic about his vacuum cleaners for me not to be a little skeptical. I have to admit, however, that it is the best vacuum cleaner I have ever used and I wouldn't hesitate to buy another one if the need arose.

While both of these vacuum cleaner companies relied on some pretty aggressive sales tactics, they both offered products that lived up to their claims. People don't mind being sold. What they don't like is feeling cheated.

This is why so many people dislike the process of buying a new car. I'd rather have a tooth pulled without the benefit of anesthesia than go to the car lot. The fact that the dealer makes a lot of money or that the salesmen are pushy is not what bothers me. What really bothers me is knowing that the next guy to walk into that showroom just may negotiate a better deal than I got if he's aggressive enough.

Sometimes the product, not the price, is the source of the distrust. When I started my career, I purchased all of my dress shirts from a particular mail order company. I enjoyed the convenience of shopping by mail, and I knew from experience that the shirts were of excellent quality. I was a loyal customer.

Over time, however, I noticed that the quality began to deteriorate noticeably. The price was the same as it had always been, but the company obviously began to cut corners in order to hold that price. I eventually stopped doing business with them because I didn't want their shirts at *any* price. I would gladly have paid more to get the shirt I was accustomed to, but they were no longer selling that shirt.

Unfortunately for that company, I didn't just stop buying dress shirts. I also stopped buying other things from them. I felt I could no longer trust them. They had, in my opinion, tried to pull the wool over my eyes, and no customer should put up with that for long.

Good Trees, Good Fruit

The lesson to take from all this is the same lesson offered in the simple story of a tree and its fruit. In business, as in life, good trees produce good fruit and bad trees produce bad fruit. Which of the two your company is will be up to you and the others who work there. Whichever you choose, however, your choice will eventually become apparent in the marketplace.

Every business revolves around its people. And there can be a lot of them. The Fortune 500 companies employ approximately thirty million in total. The top twenty-five alone employ nearly five million. A few bad apples, as they say, can take a lot of people down with them. Just ask the twenty thousand people who worked at Enron before its collapse.

How do you separate the good from the bad before they do something unethical or illegal, or before they prove unable to do the job you expected them to do? That, of course, is the question business has been struggling with since the first commercial exchange was made. It is the primary question society at large has dealt with since Adam and Eve left the Garden of Eden.

There is no simple answer to that question. But I've hired and promoted a lot of people, and sometimes have had to reverse a bad decision, so I've accumulated a few guidelines that have worked well for me. They're not foolproof, and I'm the first to admit I've made exceptions to my own rules. On balance, however, I believe my approach is as good as any and better—and certainly cheaper—than most.

As I argued in the last chapter, I believe it's a huge mistake to assume that you can measure job performance to any meaningful degree. That doesn't mean that people shouldn't be held accountable or that their fate shouldn't be tied to the fate of the organization. It does mean you should never hire anyone based solely on the accomplishments listed on his or her resume.

I believe in hiring people based on four criteria. They are, in order of priority:

Character
Motivation
Experience
Accomplishments

Character

Every employee is an ambassador for the company. A job is a 24/7 matter. That doesn't mean I expect people to work around the clock. In fact, I'm skeptical of people who spend too much time at the office. I prefer to work with people who have a life. They're a lot more interesting and, in my experience, a lot more effective.

The case for character could not be more important. At some point down the road each one of your colleagues will face the choice of putting a knife in your back or helping you and the company through a problem. Do you want that person to be brilliant and self-serving or capable and trustworthy when the time comes?

Blind loyalty is not what you want in any employee. The further you rise up the organization, the more you will rely on others for information. Those who won't tell the emperor that he is wearing no clothes, as the old tale goes, do the emperor and the company a disservice.

When I was a company president I could be very persuasive. That wasn't always good for me or the company, though. On one occasion, the management group was split over a very contentious issue. I was in the office of one of the senior officers explaining my reasoning for taking the position I had and trying to solicit his support. After a while, he said, "I'm not going to try to debate you on this, because I know I won't win. You have the gift of debate and you're the boss. I'll ask you only one question: Do you need to win every argument?"

He didn't expect an answer and I didn't give him one, but I sure thought a lot about his insightful question. I concluded that I did enjoy winning a debate, but that debating with the people who worked for me wasn't really a fair debate anyway. I went back to the people who disagreed with me and, for the first time, really listened to their arguments. I didn't abandon my position completely, but I did abandon my intransigence.

Integrity is at the heart of character. People of integrity ultimately make the best decisions. The reason is simple. They've already decided what they are and they can put all of their effort into making the right decision. They don't have to go through all kinds of mental gymnastics about which decision will benefit them the most. They've already decided that doing the right thing is more important than doing the self-serving thing.

Related to this, nothing has annoyed me more in recent years than the idea that companies in trouble should pay "retention bonuses" to executives as an incentive to keep them from jumping ship while the company works out its problems. If they aren't the type of executive who would see the company through simply because it's the honorable thing to do, they shouldn't have been hired in the first place. There was a time when a senior executive would have been ashamed to show his face at his family's Thanksgiving table if he had bailed out of a sinking ship.

The CEO at the helm of Kmart when it went into bankruptcy had been with the company for just a couple of years. The story goes that when he first arrived at headquarters, he issued an order to remove the portraits of his predecessors that were hanging on the walls, saying something to the effect that he didn't care much about history. I believe the board should have relieved him of his duties right then and there. He had played the hand of the person he really was—petty and narcissistic.

Character is a tough quality to measure. I came up with a simple litmus test, however, that seems to work pretty well. I prefer to interview job candidates at lunchtime. It gives me a chance to talk with them in a less formal setting than my office. But more importantly, I like to take them to the cheapest restaurant in town, what some might call a "hole-in-the-wall." It's not that I'm frugal. I want to see how they treat the person who serves us. If they are arrogant and snooty and act as if their time is more valuable than that of the person serving us, I generally won't hire them. If, on the other hand, they are considerate, they clear the first hurdle. The way a person treats someone who is in an "inferior" position is a good sign of what character they have and what kind of colleague they will be.

Motivation

Hiring the most brilliant business person in the world is a huge mistake if he is not motivated to apply his brilliance to your company. Again, it's not that you want people who are going to spend all of their waking hours at the office. You don't. But you do want people who are willing to spend the night filling sandbags when the river starts to rise.

Motivation provides purpose, and purpose provides context. If we don't have a context for our actions, our actions are likely to lose steam over time. Motivation is directly related to character. A good employee is someone who is what she appears to be. If someone is hiding who she is from view, she'll eventually hide other things, which might put the company at the precipice of a real problem. Such honesty is a critical element of character, and is inherent in a well-motivated colleague.

As a twenty-something manager, I was challenged by the executive in charge of a downsizing program for not terminating a certain individual who most people considered to be a bit of a slacker. I admitted that I had given it a great deal of thought and concluded that if this guy wasn't putting in a full day's work, it was our fault for not giving him a full day's work. I believed he was a person of character with an underdeveloped sense of motivation. We revised his job description, and over time he became a critical member of the department. The executive who suggested I should let him go admitted that it would have been a big loss if I had followed his suggestion and ignored my gut feeling about our colleague's character and ability to be motivated.

It wasn't that I was any smarter about people than this executive. In many ways, just the opposite is true. The difference between us at the time was that he looked at what the man had done, and I looked at who he was and what he could do. He was good fruit, as the story goes, that simply appeared to have produced a bad crop at the time.

Experience

Experience is important, although at number three on my list it is not the most critical. I classify experience as a "get it if you can" quality—nice to have, but not a deal-breaker in my decision to hire someone.

As company president, I once had to replace my executive assistant, who was retiring after a lifetime of employment with the company. She had big shoes to fill, but I ultimately chose a woman who had limited experience as an executive assistant. The reason I hired her was that when I asked her if there was anything about being an executive assistant that she really didn't like to do, she told me that the last person she had been an assistant to was having an affair and had asked her to lie about his whereabouts when his wife called. She said it had made her very uncomfortable and that she had vowed not to compromise her values again. I knew she was my kind of people and she got the job. I never regretted the decision.

Accomplishments

That brings me to the least important criterion for evaluating people in the workforce—or any place else, for that matter. I choose never to judge people on the basis of their past accomplishments. I'm not suggesting that a person's past actions don't provide *any* evidence of future behavior or performance. I do believe, however, that we've taken the concept of granting opportunity on past achievement to an illogical and unhealthy extreme.

Published authors will tell you that the most difficult career challenge was getting anyone to look at their work before they were published. Stephen King said in a radio interview that he had worked in an industrial laundry for several years before anyone would publish his work. Every writer runs into the same thing—you can't *get* published until you've *been* published.

What is the logic of that? If you've been published, theoretically, at least one other editor has looked at your work and liked it. But what if that editor didn't know what he was talking about or just happened to be your brother-in-law? At some point in their career, none of the great authors had been published, and they were the same writers who ultimately became famous.

In the academic community, past accomplishments are very important. You won't get a job at a prestigious university if you don't have a lengthy and impressive curriculum vitae. But aren't there people who are very good at getting degrees who may not be very good teachers? I would think so, just as I'm sure there are some people who would make excellent teachers who would not even be considered for the opportunity because they don't have an advanced degree or haven't acquired the right credentials.

History is full of individuals like Abraham Lincoln, who, after an incredible string of personal failures, went on to change the world for the better. Those individuals, unfortunately, would probably not have the same opportunity to contribute today. Particularly in business, we worship accomplishment and don't tolerate failure. Our accomplishments, however, will mean nothing at the end of the day. As the parable makes clear, a good tree bears good fruit, not pretense and false appearance, which are of no bearing to God. We will be judged on the basis of the people we are and the purpose we have lived for.

For Further Review

What is your experience with truth? Does it always come out?

Are you the person you appear to be? Explain.

What makes a person "good fruit"?

Do you know anyone that Jesus would consider an "evildoer"?

How do you evaluate people?

In what ways does your company value character?

What motivates you?

Would you like to pursue a new vocation but feel trapped for lack of relevant experience?

Do your past failures portray the real you?

How will God judge you?

Chapter 9.

Taking Chances

The Parable of the Talents

J esus said, "Again, it will be like a man going on a journey, who called his servants and entrusted his property to
them. To one he gave five talents of money, to another
two talents, and to another one talent, each according to his
ability. Then he went on his journey. The man who had received
the five talents went at once and put the money to work and
gained five more. So also, the one with the two talents gained
two more. But the man who had received the one talent went
off, dug a hole in the ground and hid his master's money.

"After a long time the master of those servants returned
and settled accounts with them. The man who had received
the five talents brought the other five. 'Master,' he said, 'you
entrusted me with five talents. See, I have gained five more.'

"His master replied, 'Well done, good and faithful servant! You have been faithful with a few things; I will put
you in charge of many things. Come and share your master's happiness!'

"The man with the two talents also came. 'Master,' he said,
'you entrusted me with two talents; see, I have gained two more.'

"His master replied, 'Well done, good and faithful servant! You have been faithful with a few things; I will put
you in charge of many things. Come and share your master's happiness!'

"Then the man who had received the one talent came. 'Master,' he said, 'I knew that you are a hard man, harvesting where you have not sown and gathering where you have not scattered seed. So I was afraid and went out and hid your talent in the ground. See, here is what belongs to you.'

"His master replied, 'You wicked, lazy servant! So you knew that I harvest where I have not sown and gather where I have not scattered seed? Well then, you should have put my money on deposit with the bankers, so that when I returned I would have received it back with interest.

"'Take the talent from him and give it to the one who has the ten talents. For everyone who has will be given more, and he will have an abundance. Whoever does not have, even what he has will be taken from him. And throw that worthless servant outside into the darkness, where there will be weeping and gnashing of teeth'" (Matthew 25:14-28).

The parable of the talents teaches us that God wants each of us to use all of the abilities he has bestowed upon us. God wants us to know him, and we can use our talents to their fullest only if we do. We simply can't do it alone.

Realizing Our Potential

Some people view our need to know God as a prerequisite to realizing our full potential as a form of reliance upon God's power. It is, of course, but that perspective misses a key point. Even with faith, God is not going to *make* us successful. He isn't going to give us the answers to the test beforehand or let us see the future so we can get rich in the stock market. We will have to work for our success. God will help, but the effort has to be our own.

One of the reasons we can't realize our full potential in life without God's help is that we must know him in order to understand *ourselves* fully. We are God's creation. Who we are and what we can achieve cannot be isolated from who he is and his plan for us.

If we are working on our relationship with God, the hard work it will take to realize our potential will not seem like work at all. Our work will then have purpose and we will do it joyfully. Even more importantly, when we center our lives on our relationship with God, our accomplishments become measurable and the more we succeed, the more successful we become.

A friend of mine frequently observes that "Them that has, gets." What she's typically referring to is the fact that if you go to a sporting event or a concert, the people who could most easily afford to buy tickets are the ones most likely to be given them for free. A similar phenomenon applies to Christian faith. Faith in Jesus Christ motivates us to do our best. That, in turn, gives us motivation to do even better. And with such powerful motivation we can usually succeed. "Them that has, gets."

Do you believe you can measure your success by the money and possessions you've accumulated? You can't. First of all, as I pointed out in an earlier chapter, no matter how much money you have, somebody always has more. You can't keep up with the Joneses because a new family perpetually occupies the Jones house and each one has more "things" than the last.

More importantly, even if you have more than the Joneses temporarily, someone can take it all away tomorrow. Think of the major historical events of the last five hundred years. Whether these milestone events involved revolution or war or ethnic or religious intolerance, the one thing common to all of them is that somebody lost the "things" they had acquired.

Material possessions are a measure of power as much as accomplishment, and power and accomplishment are two very different things. Power is the ability to take something.

Accomplishment represents the ability to earn it. Either way, however, material possessions are inanimate and self-contained. They can be taken by force. And eventually, they must be left behind.

Will your wealth at least bring you comfort? To an extent, yes. After your basic needs are satisfied, however, greater comfort provides rapidly diminishing incremental pleasure or satisfaction. A house is a house. A car is a car. A shower curtain is a shower curtain.

I have always lived in the northern part of the United States. Like some northerners, I sometimes go south in search of sunshine during those long grey months. And one thing I've observed on all of those searches for warmth and sunshine is the large number of people who live in the midst of it and appear to take the beautiful weather for granted. They often don't even appear to notice a beautiful day. Instead of going to the beach on a day that northerners are dreaming of, they will frequently find an excuse to stay inside.

I once had the chance to build the house of my dreams high up on a hill overlooking a beautiful rolling valley. I worked closely with the architect to make sure that I could enjoy that view from every room in the house. There simply couldn't be too many windows. After living in my dream house for a while, however, I stopped noticing the beautiful view. It lost its impact. The view hadn't changed, but it had become a routine sight. I stopped seeing it for what it was. People would visit for the first time and marvel at how wonderful it must be to live with such a spectacular view. In reality, I was more aware of the fact that the wind on top of the hill was constantly blowing shingles off the roof than I was aware of the beautiful view.

Do you play golf? Have you ever seen a happy golfer? There aren't that many of them, and even when they are happy, it's usually a fleeting sensation. Everybody gets frustrated eventually. It's just one of those games. I think it's a great game, but I'm not particularly adept at it, so I'm frequently frustrated. That is why I'm always surprised at how disappointed very good golfers are when they get *only* a par on a hole that they believe they should have birdied. I would be jumping up and down with a par, but they sulk off to the next tee as if they had just made a double bogey.

The point of these analogies is that the comfort and satisfaction that you believe wealth will bring you is illusory. Whatever happiness it brings will be temporary. That's not to say that wealth is evil. Wealth is *nothing.* It acquires meaning only as a result of what you do with it.

The same goes for talent. Talent is worth nothing if, like the third servant in the parable, we simply bury it in the yard and preserve it. No one will ever remember how much unapplied talent we had. There are no listings in any encyclopedia for people who were marvelously talented but never once demonstrated it. No one has ever made the nightly news for being the most talented person on Earth to do nothing that day.

God doesn't simply value our talent, either. He cares only what we do with it. This is why the servant who turned two talents into four in the parable got the same warm reception from his master as the servant who turned five talents into ten. One servant may have had more ability than the other, but that's not what the master was testing. The master wanted to know which servant or servants would utilize their talents to the fullest on the master's behalf.

Utilizing talents isn't the same as having "a lot of heart." Having heart, as the phrase is frequently used today, simply means refusing to give up. That's a great quality to have, but we can persevere for a lot of reasons that have nothing to do with either character or faith. Some people persevere out of fear. Others persevere out of envy or jealousy. Neither has anything to do with talent.

Purpose

Purpose is also important to God. For what purpose do you utilize your talents? Is it for fame? If so, you'll be disappointed. As television's Dr. Phil says, "You wouldn't care so much about what people think of you if you knew how seldom they actually did."

I've had the chance in my business career to be around some celebrities. It's fun to walk into a fully booked restaurant without a reservation and have the restaurant manager actually bring out an additional table so that your party can be seated immediately. And it's hard not to think that the celebrity aura spills over onto you and the other members of the group. Once you've been around it for a while, however, you realize that celebrity is an emotional jail. Most of the people who want a celebrity's autograph or who whisper to their friends about a celebrity that walks by aren't admiring the celebrity at all. They're admiring the fact that they're in the presence of a celebrity—that they now have an interesting story to tell their friends. In other words, the excitement that onlookers may feel in the presence of a celebrity has more to do with the onlookers than with the celebrity. The celebrity is just a tool.

In the same way, business is just business. The most successful business in the world will, in the end, be of no value. The only thing that will matter is whether, in making that business, we utilized all of the talent God gave us, and whether we directed it toward the right purpose—our relationship with God.

A teaching pastor told me of a church member who once asked him if it was okay to pray for more sales for his company. The question suggests that if God is inclined to answer your prayers, he will *grant* the company more sales. He won't. God doesn't write orders. Only the people who work at the company can make a sale.

By praying to God, however, we become closer to him. That gives us the strength of knowing him, and that may well lead to more orders. If we can turn the strength of knowing God into more productive effort, in other words, we just might achieve what we're praying for in the first place.

What is talent? It is the ability to do something that, by implication, most people can't. No one is said to have a talent for breathing or growing toenails. These are just things we all do. We also typically associate talent with abilities that we admire and that do some good. We might say that someone has a talent for sports if he is a good athlete, but few of us would say, except perhaps ironically, that a bank robber has a talent for theft.

In a sense, talent is simply the way by which we realize God's plan for us. God has a plan for everyone and each one is different. If we succeed in satisfying his plan for us, we have, by definition, succeeded in using our talent. This is why it is an affront to God not to use the talent he has given us. If we don't use it, we cannot achieve God's plan.

Our Talents and Our Risks

Why do you suppose God doesn't just tell us what his plan for us is? Why aren't we born with an instruction manual that tells us what God wants us to do with our lives? For the same reason that the master in the parable of the talents didn't leave instructions with his servants on what to do with the money he had left with them.

Fulfilling God's plan for us is not a homework assignment. Teachers assign homework in order to teach. God's plan for us, by contrast, is both the means by which we use our talents and the end toward which we apply them. In achieving God's plan for us, we earn his respect and we earn the eternal reward of knowing him.

The process by which we make the most of our talents, therefore, always involves discovery. And since discovery is, by definition, the acquisition of something previously unknown, there is always a certain amount of risk involved. We can't fulfill God's plan for us without taking some chances.

Sometimes the risk involves the discovery of other talents. I have a childhood friend who suffered a traumatic skiing accident at the age of nineteen. He was the most expert and graceful skier I had ever seen; I still have not seen his equal. But after the accident he would never walk again. A natural athlete, he faced a life without the benefit of the one talent that had taken precedence over all others since birth.

It would have been easy to give up hope, and I'm sure there were many times when he came close, but he didn't. He began to discover new talents that he hadn't previously been aware of. Now, some thirty years later, he has a great marriage, a successful career, and a solid relationship with God. He overcame not by giving up risk, as might have been natural after such an accident, but by taking more risks, ultimately discovering that God's plan for him had little to do with skiing and everything to do with attitude and purpose.

Risk, even when things seem to be going well, is also an inherent part of business. As most business people instinctively realize, there seldom comes a time when you can just sit back and let the business run itself. Even if there is little noticeable change in your marketplace, you must constantly get better at what you do. If you don't, someone else will, and will eventually take your customers away.

One of my favorite movie scenes comes from the 1988 movie *Tucker: The Man and His Dream*. Tucker was an entrepreneur in the late 1940s who had an idea for a stylish new car, and is trying to convince the management of the Ford Motor Company to build it. A young Henry Ford II, best known for turning the formerly entrepreneurial company into a modern business, is in charge at the time. Once Tucker finishes his pitch for his revolutionary new design, Henry Ford II turns him down with the explanation that he's not going to risk the company on a single car. It would simply be too risky for a modern company to consider. The original Henry Ford, however, now an old man, appears to have different thoughts on the matter. From the other end of the table, he breaks in to Henry II's explanation with the comment, "This company was *built* on one car!"

Conceptually, that's true of every company. Wal-Mart began with one store. Intel began with one computer chip—for a calculator. One of the early predecessors of IBM began with one time clock. Not one of them was destined to become the titan it ultimately became. Each did so only because the company was willing to take risks.

Could the servant given the five talents by his master have lost everything in the process of turning five talents into ten? Of course. The only option to accepting some degree of risk, however, was to bury the talents, as the third servant did. As the parable teaches, the safety of such a risk-avoiding strategy is illusory. There were consequences for doing nothing, not rewards like those given the servants who took risks.

There is no way to avoid all risk. Risk is an inherent element of life, and business is just a facet of life. Risk is as much a part of business as are the economic cycles in which it operates. Risk affects us even when we try to avoid it. Avoidance, in fact, often magnifies the actual risk we face.

Resilience and Patience

Does that mean we should bet our business at every opportunity, that we should chase the risk that could cause our business to collapse? Obviously not. There may be times when that level of risk is unavoidable, but such times are very rare. Few companies really stand at the precipice of extinction, and those that are at the point that a huge gamble represents the only chance of survival have typically come to that point over a long period of time.

My neighbors think I'm a pretty good gardener, so they sometimes approach me when they have plant-related questions. I love to be outside in the summertime and find flower gardening to be a great way to relax. Our yard has quite a few flowers and is generally well-maintained.

In reality, I know very little about gardening. I've never read a book or taken a class. I can seldom tell you the name of a plant, even if it's in one of our flowerbeds. What I do have, however, is the willingness to try things. I've learned through experience that plants are actually pretty resilient and there's a wide margin of error in growing them. That's not true of all plants, of course, but enough of them to give you a colorful yard.

Have you ever noticed that the best cooks are seldom precise in measuring out ingredients? The key to great cooking is the willingness to try things. It's actually pretty hard to mess up most basic meals. It can be done, but I've been pleasantly surprised at how well my experiments turn out most of the time.

In business, the most common mistake I see when it comes to trying new things is a lack of patience. There's an inclination to want to "cut your losses" when things aren't happening as quickly as you would like or had planned. Time and time again, companies pull the plug on projects that are just on the verge of paying off.

Impatience in business is really just a variation of preoccupation with change. As I argued earlier, change seldom occurs as quickly as business people are inclined to believe it will, even in our current age of "rapid change." But when we want change and it doesn't come quickly, we start to believe it's never going to happen.

In the end, talent doesn't guarantee anything. Even Tiger Woods has a bad round of golf from time to time. If we don't push the limits of our talent we will never discover where those limits are. Even more importantly, it is the act of discovering the extent of our talents that brings us closer to God. Our talent is the means by which we achieve God's plan for us. It's meant to be applied, not buried for safekeeping.

For Further Reflection

Which of the servants in the parable of the talents are you most like?

What is talent, as the word is used today?

What talents do you possess?

What would you like to pray for, but don't? Why not?

What would life be like if someone took all of your possessions away?

When was the last time you really took a chance? How did it turn out?

What do you take for granted?

Does your boss encourage you to develop your talents?

Will God be pleased with what you have done with your life?

What is God's plan for you?

Chapter 10.

Perspective Revisited

Parable of the Rich Fool

Someone in the crowd said to him, "Teacher, tell my brother to divide the inheritance with me." Jesus replied, "Man, who appointed me a judge or an arbiter between you?" Then he said to them, "Watch out! Be on your guard against all kinds of greed; a man's life does not consist of the abundance of his possessions."

And he told them this parable: "The ground of a certain rich man produced a good crop. He thought to himself, 'What shall I do? I have no place to store my crops.'

"Then he said, 'This is what I'll do. I will tear down my barns and build bigger ones, and there I will store all my grain and my goods. And I'll say to myself, "You have plenty of good things laid up for many years. Take life easy; eat, drink, and be merry."'

"But God said to him, 'You fool! This very night your life will be demanded from you. Then who will get what you have prepared for yourself?'

"This is how it will be with anyone who stores up things for himself but is not rich toward God" (Luke 12:13-21).

In responding to the man who asks Jesus to force the man's brother to share an inheritance, Jesus does not denounce the wealthy brother for not sharing. The parable Jesus tells takes a strong position on the matter of wealth, but Jesus makes it clear that this brotherly dispute over an inheritance is not for him to resolve.

Is Jesus saying that God is the only legitimate judge, or is he suggesting that God does not wish to arbitrate worldly matters between men? Wouldn't life be so much easier if God would intervene whenever we feel we've been wronged?

There's an old proverb that says, "Give a man a fish and he will eat for a day; teach him to fish and he will eat for a lifetime." Like that old proverb, Jesus is telling us that when it comes to disputes between people, God would rather teach us to find solutions than dictate them from on high.

A Matter of Perspective

More than anything else, this is a parable about perspective. How an inheritance is divided up between two brothers is not of great interest to God. God is interested, however, what each brother does with his inheritance, and that is a matter of the perspective each brother has on his possessions and material wealth.

Whatever we do with our lives, God will still be God. We know we can't buy our way into God's kingdom. God doesn't want our money or our possessions. God is not impressed by barns full of food and drink. Money and possessions are of this world, and as we've all observed, we can't take them with us.

In the parable of the rich fool, Jesus is telling us that the things we accumulate in life are relevant only to the extent we are "rich toward God." And that is a matter of perspective.

Perspective is critical to faith. When we stray, it is frequently a loss of perspective that leads us away from the proper path. We lose sight of our real objective, our real purpose. Without purpose, as I've noted repeatedly, there is no context for right and wrong. If it doesn't matter where we're going, anything goes.

By the same token, life clearly isn't fair if we have no context for measuring opportunity other than the extent of our possessions. In the words of Jesus, "Man, who appointed me a judge or an arbiter between you?" We all live at various levels of material comfort. God isn't going to intervene. That doesn't mean he doesn't want *us* to do something about it. It simply means that material inequity is of our making, and it is up to us to work it out.

But we all have the same opportunity to know God. The person who has nothing has no less a chance to know God that the person who owns the fertile ground or the factory. Both have the same opportunity to succeed or fail in life if we calibrate success and failure by the standards of our relationship with God. That's all that really matters in the end, which, as the parable teaches, may come at any time.

The end could come tonight. It could come in five minutes. Will I be ready? Will I have my spiritual affairs in order, or have I been putting off developing my relationship with God until my work slows down and my kids are grown?

We all have priorities, but we too often plan our lives in phases, as if each phase is somehow distinct. The man in the parable is in a happy phase—he has plenty of good things in storage. He will take life easy; eat, drink, and be merry.

Faith is a matter for every day, here and now, not to be put off until a more convenient time, not to be stockpiled like a good harvest. Making faith a daily priority is the perspective that keeps us on the path.

Perspective on Our Work

One of the saddest facts about modern life is that so many people dislike their work. Too many people can't wait to quit or retire, to walk away from the unfulfilling drudgery and stress of their job. It's a reality that's undoubtedly good for lottery ticket sales, but is an unfortunate and unnecessary way to live.

At the age of nineteen, I decided to see some of this great country of ours, so I left New England and headed to California. I found work in the lush agricultural region south of San Francisco as a laborer for a company that made vinegar for salad dressing. I was assigned to a three-person crew with two other young men about my age. They were from Mexico. They spoke no English, and I didn't understand a word of Spanish. All three of us were in a foreign country.

The work was hot, dirty, and physically strenuous. That job, however, had a profound impact on me because of what I learned from my co-workers, starting on our first day on the job. When they reported to work at 5 AM, they would lay tortillas over the top of the steam pipes to warm them up for the morning break. When the break came, they removed the tortillas and spooned in a filling that had been prepared the night before and stored in a heat-retaining canister.

On the first day, I rested nearby on a pile of sacks while they prepared their snack. When the first tortilla was ready, one of the young men got up and brought it over to me. Totally unprepared for this, I waved my hand in the universal gestures of thanks and decline. He wouldn't give up, though, and my second co-worker also gestured that I should take it and join them. I accepted, we ate together, and that became our morning ritual.

These were two of the happiest young men I have ever met. Unlike the kids I had grown up with, many of whom spent a good deal of time complaining about what they didn't have and envying others with more, these two guys were completely focused on what they *did* have, which from their perspective was everything that really mattered. They were surrounded by friends and family who loved them; they had food in their bellies, a roof over their head, a steady job, and the opportunity to sit at God's side.

I was receptive to the lesson of their example because my parents had taught me the dignity of all work. It is not an exaggeration to say that they taught me to *enjoy* the most menial of chores. How people respond to work, they taught me, speaks volumes about their character and their life-perspective. For example, when I was eight years old, we moved into a new neighborhood. My brother was four years older and it was our job to mow the lawn with an old-fashioned manual mower. The first time we mowed the lawn at the new house, the woman who lived next door saw us and felt sorry for us. She came over and offered our father the use of her modern power mower. My father thanked her for the offer, but declined. "That's very kind of you," he said, "but I already have *two* power mowers."

In business, we often make it difficult for all employees to find dignity in their work. We tend to overlook those workers on the bottom rungs of the ladder, and even worse, we constantly *remind* them that their place is at the bottom. We even demean them if they somehow find pride and purpose in what they do.

We build the workplace culture today around the idea of "getting ahead" rather than "being satisfied." We motivate workers to move on rather than to make the most of the role they play. We make it clear that if they aren't being promoted they are somehow failing.

At every company, one of the most important employees is the individual who greets visitors. At that moment in time, they are the face and the attitude of the entire company. Frequently, however, they are one of the most poorly compensated, least-trained, and seldom-acknowledged employees in the company.

It's yet another example of our preoccupation for measuring and ranking everything. What is really gained by assigning job grades to every job, other than to remind the people in the jobs ranked in the lower grades that their jobs are considered unimportant—that they are "unskilled"? We need to assign wage levels on a consistent and objective basis, to be sure, but that can be accomplished without a detailed grade matrix that, more than anything else, serves to remind employees who's in charge—and that they are not.

Marking Time

In a similar way, companies tend to lose perspective on time. They do a lot of planning for the future, make some effort to dissect the past, but show little concern for what's going on *today*. Many employees are directed to spend more time planning than carrying out actual tasks. It makes business appear to be much more complicated than it really is and causes companies to tie up vast resources with little benefit.

The best example of this loss of perspective comes from the area of production scheduling and inventory management. As manufacturing became more automated in the middle of the twentieth century, production machines became faster but required more time to prepare for production. There were usually complex tools involved that took a lot of time to get in place and properly adjusted before production could actually begin.

As a result, manufacturers spent a lot of time and effort developing formulas to tell them exactly how many pieces to run at one time. Obviously, once the machine was set up, it could typically knock out a lot of pieces in a short period of time, and running more than you needed saved the time and cost of setup in the future. On the other hand, the raw materials and parts that went into that production had to be paid for when used, so no company wanted products sitting around for too long before they could be sold, shipped, and billed to customers.

As sophisticated as those run-size formulas became, however, the effectiveness of these calculations ultimately turns on something that is almost impossible to predict with any accuracy—the future demand for the product. Despite spending large amounts of time and money developing complex statistical techniques for forecasting future demand, companies invariably got it wrong. They would end up with too few or too many parts which, either way, cost money.

At some point, Japanese manufacturers such as Toyota realized that companies had lost perspective on the issue. They realized that no mathematical model would ever accurately predict future customer demand for a product. So instead of trying to calculate the optimal number of pieces to produce in order to make the best use of long setup times, they focused on reducing the amount of set up time. Their goal was very simple: They wanted to make it so easy to set up the machines that it would be economical to produce every part only when, and in the quantity, they actually needed. It became known as Just-In-Time production, and it has now become the standard of world-class manufacturing.

It's a lesson straight from the parable of the rich fool: Keep the right perspective and focus on what you're doing today, not on what you plan to do in the future. Don't be drawn into the fool's game of measuring, counting, and accumulating. Set the right priorities and define all of your efforts around them.

Another area in which businesses tend to lose perspective on time is engineering, where working in the future is a way of life. It's easy to get bogged down in projects that appear to hold great promise but never actually go anywhere. They take on a life of their own, not just because the engineers working on the project have a vested interest in prolonging them, but because they are too ill-defined to shoot down.

I worked with a crusty old manufacturing executive who had the right perspective. He held annual planning meetings with the plant managers and engineers to review plans for the coming year. The last presentation on the two-day agenda was reserved for the engineering department.

A lot of engineering projects were big and complex and spanned more than one annual planning session. In some cases, however, projects seemed to be stuck in the initial study phase forever. The engineers always seemed to muster up some outward enthusiasm for continuing their study, but the manufacturing executive would invariably holler, "You can only be pregnant for so long."

There is a place in business for "blue sky" thinking. You can easily overdose on it, however. In addition to the potential cost, such "out of the box" thinking, particularly when it comes to technology, is simply too far out on the time horizon to tie up a lot of resources.

Time is a "variable-variable." That means that time itself is a variable, and the passage of time always introduces more variables. The further out into the future you attempt to plan, the less certain you can be that any of your assumptions will hold up. Even your objective may no longer be relevant.

The reason to avoid too much "blue sky" engineering goes much deeper than the low probability of ever seeing any return on your investment. If you are an established competitor in your industry, the chances are almost nil that you will make the next great technological breakthrough.

IBM didn't invent the personal computer, despite being completely committed to research and development and employing some of the brightest minds in all of industry and academia. Fairchild Semiconductor didn't invent the microprocessor. And although Xerox did invent the graphical user interface, they saw no commercial application for it and let it sit in a lab, where Apple founder Steve Jobs stumbled upon it.

Most modern innovation, in fact, has come from entrepreneurs, not established research and development departments. Contrary to what many experts have suggested, however, this isn't because entrepreneurs are more creative or free-spirited. The difference between entrepreneurs and people working for established companies is seen in their perspective on time.

In short, entrepreneurs don't have any time. They don't have the luxury of studying an idea or a problem forever. It's do-or-die. They may miss the mark, but they've got to take the shot now because there won't be a tomorrow. Behaving entrepreneurially, in other words, is not so much a function of some innate quality or personality type as it is a function of circumstances.

Established companies, in contrast, often spend too much time and effort on the future simply because they can. It's tempting to live in the future because the future is entirely of your making. It's easy to imagine, as the rich man in the parable did, a future of full barns and endless leisure. Unfortunately, the future may never come.

Perspective, particularly when it comes to time, is the cornerstone of faith. It's easy to get sidetracked by life. Temptation crouches in every corner and rationalization baits us at every turn. It's understandable that our view on things gets a little skewed.

It would be simple if God took care of everything and faith was just something we could stack up for future use, like so many pieces of firewood. Only then it wouldn't be our life, but God's; it wouldn't be faith, but obedience. By giving us the opportunity to know him, but the *choice* to decide which path to follow, God has given us the opportunity to experience life, not just endure it. By giving us the chance to be fools, he gives us the chance to be wise.

For Further Reflection

In what ways do you prefer to be "given a fish," and in what ways do you prefer to "learn to fish"?

Are you a planner? What do you plan?

What is your attitude toward work?

What does it take to be personally fulfilled?

What is your perspective toward your possessions?

Is your company focused on the things that really matter?

Do you assume that people without possessions are unhappy?

What does it take to be a good Christian?

Do you want to "get ahead" in your job? Why?

Are you rich toward God?

Chapter 11.

Staying Focused

The Parable of the Weeds

J esus told them another parable: "The kingdom of heaven is like a man who sowed good seed in his field. But while everyone was sleeping, his enemy came and sowed weeds among the wheat, and went away. When the wheat sprouted and formed heads, then the weeds also appeared.

"The owner's servants came to him and said, 'Sir, didn't you sow good seed in your field? Where then did the weeds come from?'

"'An enemy did this,' he replied.

"The servants asked him, 'Do you want us to go and pull them up?'

"'No,' he answered, 'because while you are pulling the weeds, you may root up the wheat with them. Let both grow together until the harvest. At that time I will tell the harvesters: First collect the weeds and tie them in bundles to be burned; then gather the wheat and bring it into my barn'" (Matthew 13:24-30).

Weeds are everywhere. No landscape is immune to their growth. In the metaphorical landscape of our lives it seems at times as if goodness is being choked out by evil, morality overrun by decadence. The cheaters and the undeserving seem to get ahead by stepping on the people who follow the rules.

Breaking the Rules

Corporate scandal and accounting fraud have dominated the business news in recent years. That some executives succumbed to the temptations of power and greed is not surprising. That so many people stood by and watched and even applauded these executives along the way is both shocking and indicative of the moral decline that has gripped the American workplace.

The United States now has more than two million people incarcerated in its prisons. That's 1 in every 147 Americans. More than nine million people were arrested in this country in 2001, according to FBI statistics, that's more than the total population of eleven states *combined*. Of those arrested, more than 90,000 people were arrested for "offenses against the family and children."

Rule-breaking isn't limited to hard-core and corporate criminals. Queue up on the highway before the lane closed ahead for construction is actually closed and it's sure to take you twice as long as it should to get through the construction zone because a large number of people will jump the line. Actually stop when turning left at a blinking red traffic light and you'll probably get rear-ended. Hesitate to take the last open spot in a parking lot and another driver is sure to pretend you're invisible.

It is often said that our country operates by the rule of law. Compliance with those laws, however, is largely voluntary. There are 280 million people in the United States today and only 88,000 federal and 1,019,000 state and local full-time law enforcement officers. Respect for our institutions and the people around us is essential to the recognition of our natural rights and individual liberties. Without fairness, there can be no freedom.

It appears that fairness is losing much of its original meaning. Fairness has become less a question of right and wrong and more a question of what you can get away with.

Scamming the system is accepted behavior, often cheered rather than condemned.

Clearly the "enemy" referred to in the parable of the weeds is hard at work planting weeds in our fields of wheat. How tempting it is to remove the weeds from our midst and restore the integrity of a weedless wheat field. That, however, is the role of the harvesters. We certainly don't need to encourage the weeds, but we don't want to lose our spiritual selves in the process of eliminating them. We must stay focused on God's plan for *us*.

Coexisting with Weeds

A high school teacher of mine once asked the class to define the term "weed." It seemed like a simple question that could easily be dismissed in a matter of minutes. In fact, the question sparked a long debate that became quite impassioned. Everyone in that class of teenagers had a different opinion of what a weed was. Some opinions were very scientific, while others were very symbolic. Some answers focused on the plant, while others focused on where it happened to appear.

In the end, the teacher proclaimed, "A weed is any plant that grows where you don't want it to grow. What you consider to be a weed might well be a coveted rarity to someone else." It's a lesson that is yet another variation on the importance of perspective, only in this case there is an implied element of action. A weed, after all, begs to be uprooted.

Anyone who tries to maintain a yard or a garden knows all too well that weeds grow faster than the plants you would prefer to see thrive. And while your plants need delicate care, the weeds seem to sprout from nowhere in the most unlikely places—no fertilizer or compost necessary.

The easiest way to eliminate weeds, of course, is to cover the entire area with a slab of concrete or to douse it with a chemical agent that will prevent *any* plant from growing. But these are not desirable solutions. They deprive us of the opportunity to enjoy the flowers and plants that we would like to grow.

Similarly, there is always a tendency to try to rid our environment of people who are not like us. Sometimes we isolate ourselves. Other times we try to uproot those we consider undesirable. Either way, we risk losing ourselves in the process.

If we surround ourselves with people who think exactly as we do, we had better be sure that thinking is correct. Otherwise, we will at some point get caught believing a falsehood, because no one is likely to challenge our beliefs. Ignorance may be bliss, but it is not a path to spiritual growth or business success.

If we try to stamp out the weeds, on the other hand, we risk compromising ourselves. Intolerance can be evil's most powerful weapon of temptation. As discussed in chapter 6, doing the right thing is frequently defined by the action we don't take or the emotion we don't allow to engulf us. Judgment can be nothing more than arrogance dressed up as sanctity.

The parable of the weeds teaches us that the seeds of God's enemy will be harvested and burned in the end. The seeds of God, though, will survive and be gathered into the kingdom of heaven. The harvesters will not confuse one with the other. But until the harvest, the wheat and the weeds must coexist.

Obstacles to Sharp Focus

The parable of the weeds demonstrates that in our everyday lives we must remain pure in our faith, no matter what happens around us. We must not surrender to the weeds among us; nor should we fear that the harvesters will eventually fail to know us as we really are.

In business we have a tendency to become preoccupied with what others, particularly our competitors, are doing. It often becomes an obsession that distracts us from doing the things that will make us better. Such reliance on peripheral vision may actually prevent us from becoming all that we can be.

One of the most heavily promoted management concepts of the last decade is the idea of "benchmarking." The idea is simple enough: Measure what the most successful companies are achieving and try to duplicate their results. But such exercises seldom do more than tell your own employees how little confidence you have in them.

First of all, benchmarking assumes that you can measure whatever it is you're benchmarking. Often, you're kidding yourself. If you think you can measure customer satisfaction from a phone survey, for example, you're mistaken. Most American adults don't tell their spouse what they're really thinking. Why should they tell their inmost thoughts to people who invade their privacy, read from a script, and make it clear from their tone that they really don't care about the respondent or his opinion?

The second problem with benchmarking is that there's an assumption that you understand cause and effect. What good does it do you to know how long it takes other companies to ship customer orders if that's not really what matters to the customer for your product? If the same variables don't drive both businesses, you might as well benchmark the annual rainfall in New Guinea.

I have yet to discover two companies that are identically positioned. There are too many variables involved, so it just doesn't happen. Brands may be interchangeable to the customer, but that doesn't mean they're identical. The vulnerability to substitution simply indicates that the differences are not meaningful to the customer.

This is why, when it comes to marketing strategy or its components such as advertising, imitation isn't the sincerest form of flattery; it is the clearest form of surrender. Even if you could copy the strategies employed by your competitors, there probably isn't room in the marketplace for identical products. And if they were there first, you'll probably be the one to lose out.

That doesn't mean the first one into a new market will always win. When IBM decided to enter the personal computer market that Apple had pioneered, IBM was the one that had the established relationships with corporate information technology executives. That proved to be the "first" that mattered. When Honda started making minivans, Chrysler suffered despite having invented the category, primarily because of Honda's good reputation for quality. Kmart's decision to imitate Wal-Mart's pricing strategy, on the other hand, may have ultimately pushed Kmart into bankruptcy.

Marketing imitation often fails because the position that the imitator is trying to occupy is simply not a credible one for that company. This is a problem that is not limited to copycats, however. Any company that claims to be something it isn't will be wasting its marketing investment and probably losing customers. In the end, the marketplace always uncovers corporate insincerity and false bravado.

Is this because modern consumers are more educated consumers than their predecessors? Many experts maintain that this is the case. I believe, however, that the real change is the extent to which companies today are willing to make exaggerated claims about their company and products. Marketers are all too often so preoccupied with what consumers will respond to that they overlook the company's ability to provide it.

How many times have you heard a retailer advertise that "this is the biggest sale of the year," when in fact you know that it runs the same sale at least once a month? How can a company make quality "job one" and continually lag behind its competitors in independent customer quality ratings? (It makes you wonder how they're doing on jobs two and three.) How can so many mortgage companies all offer the lowest rate?

Puffery and Imitation

Our airwaves and ad pages are filled with exaggerated corporate claims that few people actually believe. There's even a legal name for it—*puffery*. Under the legal doctrine of corporate puffery, companies are *expected* to make exaggerated claims about themselves. That's legally acceptable, however, because it is further expected that consumers won't believe them.

Puffery explains why American consumers are, arguably, the least brand-loyal consumers in the world. Brands have lost their value in America not because consumers have wised up. I believe that consumers still *want* to be brand-loyal. Unfortunately, the brands they want to believe do not inspire loyalty.

In contrast to so much of the advertising we are exposed to today, one of the most successful advertising campaigns of all time was the U.S. campaign for the original Volkswagen Beetle. Volkswagen didn't talk about how fast, comfortable, prestigious, or sexy the car was. The car was none of these things. Their message was honest: This is an inexpensive little car that will get you where you want to go, and it will last a long time. Their animal association wasn't the cheetah or the lion that frequently star in automobile ads today, but a common bug.

Another successful advertising program of the past was the "We Try Harder" campaign developed by Avis. Former Avis CEO Robert Townsend explained that the campaign came about simply because it was the only thing they could *honestly* claim about the company. The honesty was refreshing and consumers ultimately related to the underdog positioning.

A variation of the preoccupation with benchmarking is the corporate obsession with measuring market share. As a board member, I have sat through countless hours of slide presentations in which marketing executives go into excruciating detail about how much market share each company has. They typically pay a small fortune to determine this number and waste an incredible amount of time that could have been devoted to some really productive task. Market share numbers are largely worthless.

What does it really matter if you have the most market share in an industry if, owing to other factors, you are not making money or are about to lose to a new competitor you don't see coming? What does it matter that the last promotion you ran gave your company two points of additional market share if you can't hold onto it without going broke? Without context, a company's market share says nothing about it or its prospects.

That's especially the case today because technology allows new competition to emerge from outside the established industry. The competitor you have to worry most about may currently be no more than a workbench in some entrepreneur's garage. If your established competitors don't leapfrog you in the meantime, you may ultimately be humbled by a company that you've never heard of and that never appeared on the marketing department's pie chart of market share.

The preoccupation with market share is, unfortunately, more than a harmless waste of time and money. It causes business people to think in terms of established industries with well-defined borders. Industries are rarely well-defined. If they are, they probably won't stay that way for long.

Automotive executives seem to be convinced that the market for cars and light trucks is a distinct and unique market. Most of the senior executives in this industry have spent their career in the industry and they track market share like Merrill Lynch tracks the stock market. It's not surprising, therefore, that the Detroit automakers have largely become marketing clones of one another. What one does, they all do.

If one offers zero percent financing, they all offer zero percent financing.

The incentive to imitate the competition can be strong. If we don't meet their promotional pricing, for example, we might lose sales and market share in the short term. By mimicking the competition, however, we effectively tie the company's fortunes to those of the competition. This makes life much easier for a third competitor, who now has to out-market only one competitor, not two.

If we become too focused on our competitors we will eventually begin to look and behave like them. We will lose our distinctiveness, which means that our destiny is no longer primarily in our control. As Jesus taught in the parable of the weeds, we should not become consumed with the plant beside us. It will all get sorted out in the end; it is up to us to make sure that we are the person and the business that we should be.

Organizational Myopia

Another form of poor focus that can devastate a business is organizational myopia, which causes homogeneity. Organizational homogeneity is as prevalent today as it was back when IBM required all of their male salaried employees to wear white dress shirts. If you showed up for a job interview in Silicon Valley at the height of the tech boom dressed in a conservative suit and with polished wing tip shoes on your feet, you probably didn't get hired. People who enjoyed wearing suits to work were considered too rigid and lacking in self confidence to succeed in an entrepreneurial environment.

One of the reasons behind homogeneity in business is that the people who were successful in the past inevitably become the ones to define the future. Not surprisingly, therefore, there tends to be a lot of natural continuity to the type of people who get ahead in a company. This is why, in my opinion, the glass ceiling has been so difficult for women to shatter in corporate America. It's not that the male executives—with some unfortunate exceptions—don't want women to succeed. It's that corporate America was built by men. They defined it, consciously and sub-consciously, in their own image.

Another cause of organizational homogeneity is the desire of many companies—at the urging of their consultants—to establish a corporate culture. Unfortunately, such a culture is seldom defined by shared values. More often than not it is defined by shared training and background. The tech industry wants to hire employees with tech experience; the automotive industry wants to hire people from the automotive industry; and the consumer products industry wants employees who know and understand "their" world.

There is some justification for this approach to hiring, but the practice can be self-limiting if taken to an extreme. You may end up with the best employees in the industry, but you may not end up with the best employees available. It's also likely that you will be slow to recognize and respond to change, since everyone sees what's happening through the same historical lens.

The risks inherent in organizational homogeneity become even greater when the organization is populated by individuals with homogenous personalities. We all have a need for self-validation, so we tend to look more favorably upon people who are just like us. Homogeneity is often confused with organizational culture. It gives the mistaken impression that leadership drives corporate culture, and that the attitude and personality of the senior people is adopted by everyone in the organization. That's not what happens in reality.

Even if the senior executives in an organization don't really lead by example, they do control most of the important hiring and advancement. The people they hire and promote will hire and promote the people below them, so there's a trickle-down effect that ultimately leads to a homogeneity that is commonly mistaken for culture.

Sometimes this homogeneity is actually prized. I know a CEO whose highest compliment about a new business acquaintance is, "He's just like us." That's the way he wants it. He wants to be surrounded by others who look at the world just as he does. He believes such consistency is the key to effective teamwork. He's not alone.

There needs to be some commonality among the members of any organization. They must, for example, be united in their sense of purpose and their commitment to the success of the organization. If everyone thinks alike, however, the organization is bound to make mistakes and miss opportunities.

Maintaining real diversity in an organization is a daunting task. The policies and practices of most companies stifle it. Homogeneity is rewarded and truly independent thinking is ultimately strangled. The result is an organizational environment that fails to keep everyone focused on the things that really matter. Grow your wheat and let the harvesters worry about the weeds.

For Further Reflection

What are the weeds in your wheat field?

What is your attitude toward those weeds?

Is your company honest with its customers? Explain.

In what ways do you judge others?

What brands are you loyal to? Why?

Describe your company's culture?

What values do you share with the people you work with?

In what ways is your company poorly or effectively focused?

Describe aspects of your company that demonstrate homogeneity. Do the same for diversity.

What policies could make your company more diverse?

Chapter 12.

A Life
of Achievement

The Tower of Babel

N ow the whole world had one language and a common speech. As men moved eastward, they found a plain in Shinar and settled there.

They said to each other, "Come, let's make bricks and bake them thoroughly." They used brick instead of stone, and tar for mortar. Then they said, "Come, let us build ourselves a city, with a tower that reaches to the heavens, so that we may make a name for ourselves and not be scattered over the face of the whole earth."

But the Lord came down to see the city and the tower that the men were building. The Lord said, "If as one people speaking the same language they have begun to do this, then nothing they plan to do will be impossible for them. Come, let us go down and confuse their language so they will not understand each other."

So the Lord scattered them from there over all the earth, and they stopped building the city. That is why it was called Babel—because there the Lord confused the language of the whole world. From there the Lord scattered them over the face of the whole earth (Genesis 11:1-9).

God doesn't have to worry about any modern company building a tower that reaches to heaven. Some might be inclined to try, but business people have already confused their language to the point where the necessary coordination and cooperation are impossible to achieve.

No Simple Answers

A friend once told me about a couple he knew who were new parents and who had purchased just about every book ever written on raising children. The problem for these new parents was that none of the authors agreed on much of anything. Their research into parenthood gave them more anxiety than answers.

The lack of consensus among experts is in part a reflection of the topic. Parenting is a complex subject with few absolutes. When it comes to raising children, cause and effect are frequently difficult to connect.

Another factor behind the diversity of opinion in books about parenthood has to do with publishing rather than with parenting. Publishing is a business, and a great many people write books. A potential author needs to say something new and different if he or she is to gain attention. If a company publishes books that simply repeat what everyone already believes or knows, few people will buy them and the publisher won't be able to pay its bills.

The same goes for the business management and career development categories. There are probably more "new" ideas presented in the business category than in any other, and very few of the authors seem to be in agreement. The need to stand out by being different also helps to explain how the language of business has become so overwhelmed by jargon. A lot of business executives today talk in a language that only remotely resembles any language actually used for communication. Jargon is all about making an impression, not engaging in clear communication.

I don't believe business authors deserve all of the blame for the overuse of jargon. Some of the blame has to be laid at the feet of companies that like to think they promote people on the basis of ability. A performance-driven reward system causes employees to write long, excruciatingly boring, jargon-filled reports that say little but attempt to demonstrate how much more intelligent and progressive they are than everyone else.

The Competition Trap

Problems, even crises, are sometimes created by the need for employees to prove themselves to their superiors. That's not to say that these employees are malicious or fraudulent. They're simply reacting to the performance-based reward system. To achieve a reward, they must perform; they know they won't get promoted if they don't demonstrate that they solved a problem or seized an opportunity. They're motivated, in other words, to look for monsters in the shadows, and then conquer the monster.

In the end, competition in the workplace may be a motivating factor, but if it motivates employees to create work and initiate change that may not be necessary or prudent, competition has failed. It would save time and money if companies just let employees arm wrestle for promotions. (Actually, in a way, they do so now; but it's braggadocio, not biceps, that decides the match.)

In a competitive work environment, employees can't leave well enough alone even when that would be the best strategy for the company and its shareholders. In a competition, you have to score points, and you can score points only if you do something. Not surprisingly, very successful companies often drive themselves into trouble by changing things that shouldn't be changed.

Competition is also self-limiting. To win a competition, you have only to score more points than your competitor. You don't necessarily have to perform at your highest level, which is the performance level the employer should be encouraging employees to reach.

For those who are not posturing to get ahead, there's always the need to protect one's current position. The objective of a lot of business communication today is to obscure problems, pass responsibility to a more senior level, and associate as many people as possible with a potential failure. Any communication designated "FYI" (For Your Information), for example, has the potential to be a ticking time bomb. The intent has more to do with transferal of a problem than communication for the purpose of solving the problem. E-mail doesn't help matters. Back when you had to put carbon paper into a typewriter in order to make copies, you weren't inclined to make copies without good reason. Now we can flood one another with hundreds of E-mails per day; the sheer volume will inevitably cause us to overlook the small number of messages we should actually care about.

The modern preoccupation with performance and accountability in business has also created a "flavor-of-the-month" mindset when it comes to defining the ingredients of business success. People have to prove themselves, so when they read a good business book or article they're off on a crusade to apply what they think they've learned. That is, until they read the next book or article.

I once had a boss who drove me nuts with his tendency to become consumed with the most recent business article he had read. One week he would tell me that the key to running a successful business was to be tough as nails and fire everyone who didn't produce the results we wanted. The next week he asked me how often I had lunch in the factory cafeteria and suggested that a non-confrontational relationship with employees was the best way to find out what was going on.

The Natures of Success and Failure

The hottest trend in business literature in recent years has been the empirical study of what successful companies and executives have in common. These best-selling authors are great writers. They have to be, because they have to find a story where there isn't one. The truth is that the only thing that successful companies have in common is their success. That's it! There are as many different paths to business success as there are successful companies.

Sure, successful companies do have some things in common, things that books could actually explore. These commonalities, however, are frequently not what made these companies successful. There is a phenomenon in statistics called a "coincidental relationship": two numbers that appear to be statistically related but really aren't. Business commonalities can similarly fool us with a connection that is nothing more than coincidence.

Part of the reason we're inclined to see common elements is business success is that we like to think we are in control. In reality, we often are not. In addition to assuming that personal performance is measurable, a performance-based employment system is based on the premise that business performance is a function of organizational performance. Sometimes the two are only loosely connected.

I cringe when I read a letter to shareholders in a company's annual report that refers to the CEO's strategy to build "a culture of excellence" or to create a "customer-centric culture." It's clear that the CEO is building a Tower of Babel. First of all, it arrogantly implies that people don't want to do their best or take care of the customer unless the boss leads them to these choices. Secondly, it suggests that the boss establishes the values of the organization. I reject both premises.

Psychologists tell us that human personality begins to take form at a very young age. While it can be reshaped by subsequent events in childhood and adolescence, by the time we take our first job, who we are has been largely defined. To suggest that a CEO is going to redefine the adult values of employees is ridiculous.

We also cannot ignore the contribution of the division of labor to all of this ineffective communication. Because the accountants, financial analysts, lawyers, and engineers each handle only a slice of the total business process, there's a natural competition among them to sound more informed and important than the others. Simple answers and simple questions are typically in rare supply when these groups communicate with each other, as they frequently must.

The division of labor, in theory, contributes to efficiency. Unfortunately, it also gives everyone in the organization a different stake and a different incentive. Different departments too often work at cross-purposes—assuming, of course, that they are even working on the same issues or problems.

When I was interviewing for an entry-level job in a finance department after college, the CFO who interviewed me said, "This is the best department to be in. Every decision made in this company comes down to dollars and cents, so we can stick our noses in everybody's business." I didn't realize that the head of every department was saying something similar to each of his or her job candidates—every issue comes down to a legal issue or a marketing issue or a design issue.

Most business decisions come down to all of these things, which is why so many decisions are so convoluted. In my experience, only about one in ten business decisions have come down to a simple yes or no. Many decisions are too complex for an organization to fully understand. That, of course, is to everyone's "advantage" when the autopsy is performed after a bad decision has been made. Seldom is there a single, identifiable culprit. There is safety in numbers, especially in failure.

In contrast, ownership typically isn't a problem when a decision turns out to be a good one. You probably won't even have to go looking for the owner. He or she will undoubtedly step forward voluntarily, and will probably not be alone.

Risks of Tower-Building

The commonly accepted conventions of employee compensation and advancement also contribute to the tendency of many business people to create the illusion of complexity where none actually exists. Employees are frequently compensated based on how many people they supervise, the revenues of their company or division, or the value of the assets they are theoretically responsible for. None of these variables, however, necessarily correlates to talent or effort.

Employees invariably work their hardest when the going is toughest. The most challenging management assignment I've had in my career was managing a company of one. The most I've ever had to sharpen my talents was when I started a company that had zero dollars in revenue and no assets.

What contemporary business practices do, on the other hand, is motivate everyone in the organization to build a Tower of Babel. Mid-level managers spend their time trying to get approval to hire more employees or take over additional departments. Senior managers have a great incentive to promote aggressive acquisition strategies that rarely create any lasting shareholder value. And everyone has a reason to spend money on huge investments of questionable merit.

With every mega-merger that has taken place over the last decade, and there have been many, a post-merger analysis will clearly show that there has been very little economy of scale. This is in part because scale, by definition, is a relative thing. The distance between a $10 billion company and a $50 billion company is pretty short on the scale yardstick.

A lot of the failure to meet promised cost savings in mega-mergers, however, can be attributed to the fact that every department or division sits in its own tower. When power is equated to people or assets or revenues, bigger is always going to win out over smaller. Few managers are going to step forward and voluntarily give up their power and prestige.

Another problem with promoting competition in the workplace is that everyone knows who the winners and the losers are. If management continually harps on the fact that your advancement will be limited only by your ability, and you get promoted a couple of times, you're bound to start thinking rather highly of yourself. You may even stop listening to the people you should be listening to or assuming that you have some talent that you really don't have.

If you get promoted enough, you might even begin to think you're a visionary or are somehow divined with a natural "feel" for the business. You'll start imprudently redefining the company's strategy and needlessly reorganizing its employees. You'll start, in other words, building towers to yourself.

By the same token, if you aren't ever recognized or rewarded, you're likely to lose the self-confidence you need to do any job well. Bitterness is poison to an organization. So, too, is disrespect, and it's hard to build respect among a group of people whom you openly label as winners and losers.

Self-confidence, it is said, is essential to climbing the ladder in business. Actually, that's not true. Today's most effective climbers are Babel-builders. It doesn't really matter how confident or insecure you are if you're sitting in the tallest of the many towers attempting to reach heaven.

Goals and Legacies
I frequently ask young people what their career goals are. They often answer in the way society has taught them: "I want to be a vice president" or "I want to make X amount in salary." I have always been amazed, however, at the number

of people who say that their career goal is to supervise other people.

These goals are all Towers of Babel, of course, but none is more misguided than the desire to be a boss. Believe me, it's a lousy job. When taken seriously, it is a tremendous responsibility. At best, being a boss puts you in an unnatural relationship with the people you supervise. Both sides expect too much.

Contrary to the pleasant notion that a boss can help the people who report to him or her achieve their full potential, that's an issue that each of us must work out with God, not our boss. The most supportive boss will ultimately have little effect on what his or her subordinates accomplish in life. In the end, the boss can only help people build more towers, which will bring neither the boss nor the employee much satisfaction.

People are remembered for who they are, for the character they projected. Legacy is a function of the inherent quality of what we do, not what we acquire. A single act of kindness may lead to more kindness for generations to come, allowing all of those we have touched to accomplish great things. Our money, on the other hand, may be squandered or put toward destructive behaviors. What we do lasts forever. Our acquisitions are just things.

Who is the person you remember most fondly? For me, it's my father, who died when I was a teenager. I don't remember him, however, for his title or the number of people he supervised or the amount of his salary. Chances are that the same is true for the person you remember most fondly.

The lesson is a simple one: If we are putting effort into building something that will not be meaningful to us when God calls us to his side, then it shouldn't be meaningful to us now.

God did not punish the people of Shinar because they built a tower. God will not punish us for becoming a vice president or making a lot of money. God punished the people who built the Tower of Babel because they were attempting to replace God, to put themselves above God. The ironic truth is that the people who attempted to build the Tower of Babel could not have done so without the gifts that God had given them. The same goes for us. Whatever we build, we build with the talents and the fortune that God has bestowed upon us. We do well to keep that realization at the forefront of our thoughts and actions.

W. C. Fields has been quoted as saying, "A rich man is nothing but a poor man with money." It's meant to suggest, of course, that we're all the same in the end. But that's not entirely true. The rich people have to live with the truth behind their acquisition. It can be a heavy burden, as the tale of many a wealthy celebrity will attest.

The difference between people who are personally fulfilled and those who know only inner despair is in the kind of tower they have built. Those who have built a tower in the context of their relationship with God have enjoyed a great sense of accomplishment, no matter how high their work has reached. Those who have built towers in order to usurp heaven, on the other hand, have known only the despair of the inevitable question, "Is this all there is?"

The causes of success and failure in business are many and varied. There are no hard and fast rules. Business authors will not soon run out of things to write about. There is, nonetheless, a common thread running through companies that enjoy success over a long period of time. It is the quality of humility. Successful people and successful companies do not try to build a Tower of Babel. Their sense of context makes it clear that such a project is arrogant and wasteful. They know what they have, they know what they are about, they know who is the source of their gifts and talents. And they are thankful.

For Further Reflection

Do you want to stand out from your peers? In what way?

Who do you remember most fondly? Why?

What are your career goals?

Is your compensation fair? Explain.

What is it about your job that gives you the greatest pride? The least pride?

Describe your business communication style.

Describe the legacy you would like to leave behind.

What do successful people have in common?

Is your workplace competitive? Is that good?

Are you building a Tower of Babel?

Conclusion

The key to any professional success I've achieved has been the willingness and ability to unlearn what I thought I knew about business. It astounds me still that the business knowledge that I acquired early in my career could have been so widely accepted and so wrong. I have always strived to be progressive in my thinking, but, as it turned out, I was simply following the elephant in front of me and neither one of us really knew where we were going.

My personal success (and my cup overflows with good fortune) is entirely due to my wife, Charlotte, and our hand-in-hand journey to know God. She is more than my wife and the mother of our children. She is the beacon by which I finally discovered what's important in life and how exhilarating life can be. To say that our souls are linked is to understate the depth of our relationship. She has given and she has allowed me to give.

The professional and personal facets of my life are interconnected, of course, and that is clearly one of the reasons I have been able to achieve success in both. The greatest discovery of my life has been that seeking to know God is the most stimulating and empowering reality of all.

I enjoy business. I enjoy business most, however, when it is pure, when my efforts are really about business and not about building monuments or trying to get rich or win a competition. I admit to enjoying my conquests and feeling comfortable and privileged as a result of my successes. I am no better than anyone else in that regard, and I have come to accept that about myself.

Business is life. I consider myself to be a student of life, and there is no better classroom than the world of business. I've never lacked for things to ponder and people to try to understand.

My mentor in life is my brother, a pediatric cardiologist. He looks into the eyes of very sick children on a daily basis and offers them hope and compassion. And as if that's not enough, he goes to Haiti every year as part of a church mission to share his knowledge with people who otherwise lack access to his particular expertise.

I grew up wanting to be a doctor. But eventually I decided that medicine wasn't for me. I know now that it wasn't in God's plan for me and, thankfully, I believe I realized that even before I reached out to him. Nonetheless, I believed that I could help people through my career in business. By being successful in business, I could help enable others to make a better life for themselves and their children, to provide opportunities to fulfill their God-given potential. For me, nothing could be better than that.

In 1977, when I began working for Oneida Ltd., the famous silverware manufacturer, I found that opportunity. Employees did not fear that they would lose their jobs on short notice because the company didn't make its quarterly earnings prediction. Everyone understood the need for the company to be profitable, but employees didn't believe that management was going to take any profit decline out of their hides.

We also knew that we would be allowed to fail. We could take risks without having to cover up bad decisions for fear of repercussion. We were encouraged to work with and respect our fellow employees, not to compete with them for a bigger bonus or the promotion that they really deserved. Even the boss was there to help, because he wasn't worried that some overly-eager underling would take his job.

There was also some sanity to executive compensation back then. The senior executives lived very comfortably, but they believed in fairness and self-restraint. The most highly compensated employee rarely made more than 15-20 times as much as the average worker. In corporate America today, that ratio frequently exceeds 500 to 1.

I am not proud of what my chosen profession appears to have become. Thankfully, I believe there are a lot of other business people out there who feel as I do. Despite the "weeds" we read about in the newspapers, there are still a lot of hard-working, decent people making our businesses tick.

Even so, corporate America has a long way to go to regain public trust and confidence. Just staying out of trouble won't be enough. America's companies can no longer stand on the sidelines of society and claim the excuse of globalization to justify their fixation on profits. Businesses can and must have more than one objective.

One of those objectives should be to help employees reach their full potential. Employees will not realize fulfillment if employers continue to insist that there be a thick dividing wall between the personal life and work life of employees. People of faith, in particular, will increasingly realize the limitations of the compartmentalized lifestyle. Informal groups of Christians have already formed around the country to help members find better alignment between faith and work.

As I stated in the introduction, my first objective in writing this book was to help business people find better ways to integrate what they believe and what they do for a living. One of the ways in which I've attempted to do that is by applying simple stories from the Bible to the everyday world of business. The Bible is a living document that will always say everything we need to know, no matter how we dress or how we live at the time.

The way the Bible achieves timelessness, I believe, is by offering lessons that can be interpreted on many levels. By no means do I suggest that the interpretations used here are the only interpretation, or even the doctrinally correct interpretations. I leave the doctrine to the scholars and the clergy. I pretend to be neither. I am a businessman who finds guidance in the Bible by listening to its stories and teachings and, to the best of my ability, incorporating the wisdom I find into all aspects of my daily life. It is a practice that has helped me serve God well.

The real key to integrating our careers and our faith is to understand that business is life—no more, no less. Business is not as complicated as we frequently make it out to be, and it is not constantly changing. Everything we need to know to succeed has already been written. Every situation encountered in every workday can be addressed by reading the Bible. We simply need to discern God's voice and apply the limitless knowledge God has given us.

I hope that these twelve analogies have helped form a framework for applying the Bible to lives and careers. We need never leave our faith at home. It can and should become an integral part of everything we do.

My second objective in writing *The Ultimate MBA* was to expose the fallacies in much of today's popular business thinking. The surest way to accomplish that, I believe, is by achieving my first objective. By helping people understand that business is really nothing more or less than a facet of life, I believe they will be better able to align their careers with their spiritual journey and expose the true simplicity of business.

You will have to decide whether I've accomplished one or both objectives. If I have fallen short, I sincerely apologize for taking your time. If I have succeeded, I hope you will use the knowledge to understand and fulfill God's plan for you. Know that he has one. He has one for each of us. It may require us to abandon contemporary convention and overcome fear and anxiety. If we pursue it with vigor and sincerity, however, our success is guaranteed. God has already provided us with everything we need to know. It's all right there in the Bible.